PERFECTION OF FORM shines out from the ruined columns of the Parthenon – still, **after two** thousand years, the noblest work of art created by the hand of man.

Portrait of
GREECE

Lord Kinross

Patrick Balfour

with photographs
in colour by

Dimitri

PHILADELPHIA

DUFOUR EDITIONS

1962

Printed in Great Britain for Dufour Editions

First published MCMLVI

Library of Congress Catalog Card No: 62–9152

Contents

*A chart of the major periods in Greek history is included on pp. 14 – 15,
and a map of Greece and the Islands on pp. 10 – 11.*

Plates in Colour

To

Austen Harrison

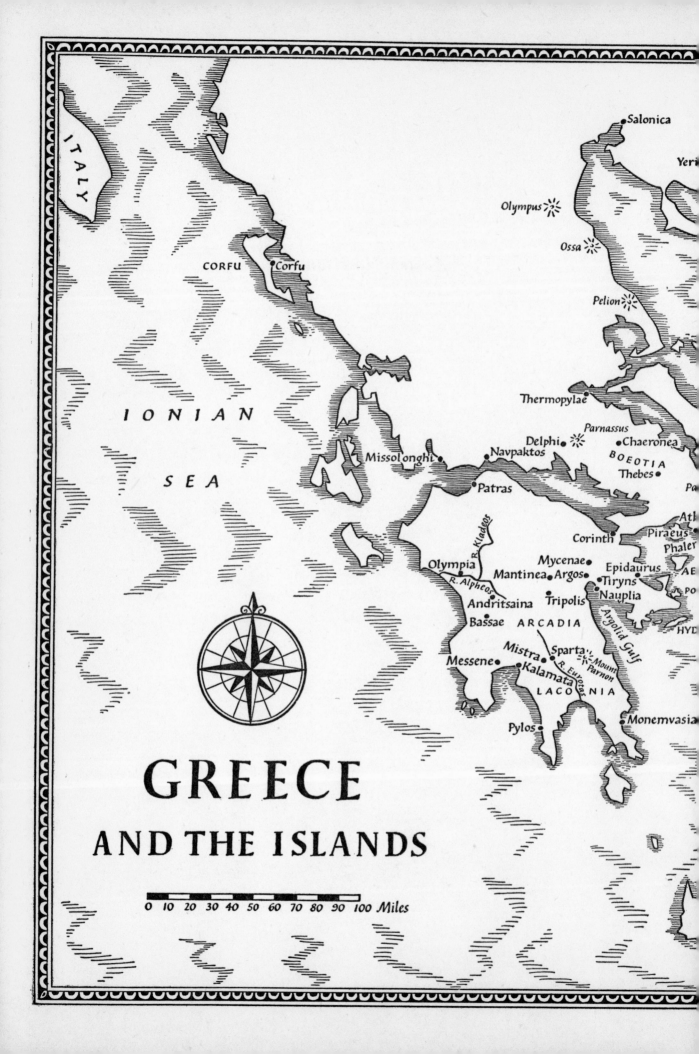

ITALY

Salonica

Yeri·

Olympus ※

CORFU · Corfu

Ossa ※

Pelion ※

IONIAN

Thermopylae

Parnassus

Delphi ※   Chaeronea

SEA

Missolonghi ·   · Navpaktos   BOEOTIA
Thebes ·

· Patras   Pa·

Corinth   Atl·
Piraeus·
Phaler·

Olympia   R. Kladeos   Mycenae·   Epidaurus   AE
Mantinea· Argos·   Tiryns·   PO·
R. Alpheos   Nauplia·
Andritsaina   · Tripolis   Argolid Gulf
Bassae·   ARCADIA   HYD·

Mistra   Sparta·   Mount
Messene·   · Kalamata   R. Eurotas   Parnon
LACONIA

Pylos·   Monemvasia·

GREECE
AND THE ISLANDS

0 10 20 30 40 50 60 70 80 90 100 *Miles*

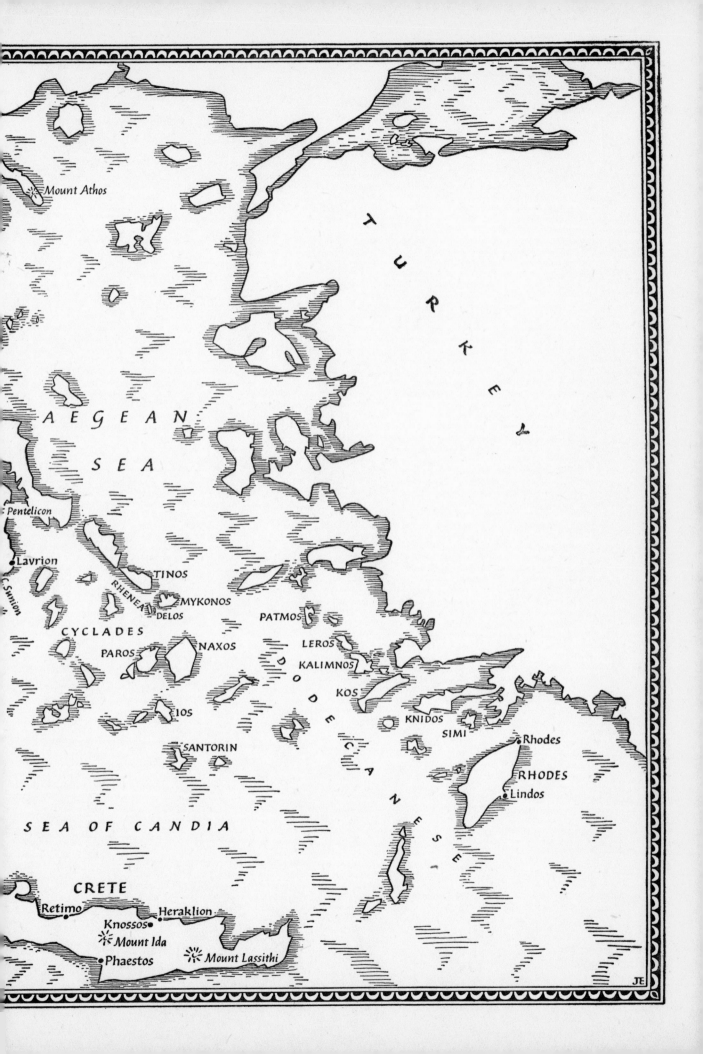

Mount Athos

TURKEY

AEGEAN

SEA

C. Pentelicon

Lavrion

C. Sunion

TINOS

RHENEA

MYKONOS

DELOS

PATMOS

CYCLADES

NAXOS

LEROS

PAROS

KALIMNOS

D O D E C A N E S E

IOS

KOS

KNIDOS

SIMI

Rhodes

SANTORIN

RHODES

Lindos

SEA OF CANDIA

CRETE

Retimo

Heraklion

Knossos

Mount Ida

Phaestos

Mount Lassithi

JE

1

The land and its story

The essence of Greece lies in its light and its landscape. The light of the Eastern Mediterranean pours down with a lucid, liquid clarity over a mountainous land, cleft into two halves and innumerable fragments by an invading, glittering sea. It is a land of islands and all but islands: peninsulas of clean, chiselled rock jutting seawards, flinging before them chains of islands reft from the parent mountains; 'peninsulas' of fertility, coiling inland, valleys and plains walled in by their massive, rough-hewn ranges. Luminous in colour, bold in form, Greece is a land without half-tones, now harsh, now luxuriant, perennially warmed by radiant sunlight and cooled by vigorous winds. Clear of the mist and the low skies, the pale diffused light and the muted tones of the Western Mediterranean, it is a land looking east, towards earlier sources of culture. It is a land which has nourished successively two of Europe's three great civilizations.

The first people known to have inhabited this world were a long-headed, non-Aryan 'Mediterranean' race, whom the Greeks called the 'people of the sea'. Mixed with them was a different, round-headed race, the people of the Anatolian continent. The centre of their world was the island of Crete, the 'Mid-Sea Land' between Europe, Asia and Africa. Here, while the Pharaohs reigned over Egypt, the Minoan Kings, semi-divine in their authority, reigned for some two thousand years over a flourishing maritime empire. Armed with perhaps the first Mediterranean navy, they commanded the coasts and the islands, kept the peace, traded with Egypt, built palaces, worshipped Anatolian gods, revered bulls, and attained to a high level of civilization in art and the amenities of living. In time they expanded over the mainland of Greece, and under the strain of this, from the fourteenth century B.C. onwards, their power declined.

It was inherited by the mainland state of Mycenae, a small principality in the Peloponnese, which grew into a major commercial and military power, dominating

not merely the islands but most of the mainland of Greece. The Mycenean kings and
their satellites built stout walled citadels, dug underground domed tombs, traded up
the Danube and even as far as the Baltic, bred horses, hunted boars, revered lions and
absorbed Minoan art and culture, giving it a distinctive touch of their own.

By now the Greeks were in the land. A people of Aryan speech, from harsher
lands, perhaps of the East, perhaps of the North, they had drifted towards the sun
and the sea, absorbing and becoming absorbed by the native race, benefiting from
its superior civilization and introducing to it their own superior language. Towards
the thirteenth century the Achaeans came, carving out settlements and kingdoms for
themselves as an aristocracy ruling native peoples, uniting to fight a war against the
Trojans, a rival power in the East which controlled the Dardanelles, profiting by
victory to extend their trade and proceed with their policy of colonial expansion in
Asia. Finally the Dorians came. A Greek people more Nordic than Mediterranean in
character, they poured down into the land rather as conquerors than as settlers, driv-
ing the Achaeans into corners of it and across the seas, destroying Mycenae and the
unity for which it once had stood, establishing a military state in the Peloponnese
and consigning the Greeks to an age of relative darkness and mutual isolation.

From this there emerged a new civilization based on a new conception of life.
The arbitrary kingdoms of Crete and Mycenae, where Kings like gods ruled over
men for their own glorification, gave place to a variety of small Greek city states,
where men ruled over themselves for their mutual benefit. In a series of transitions
from autocracy through limited monarchy, oligarchy and popular dictatorship to
democracy, the fortress and the palace gave way to the assembly and the market

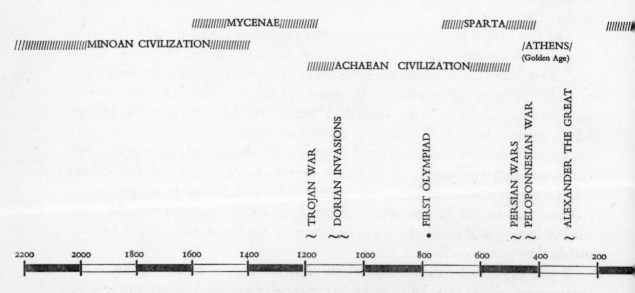

Approximate time-chart of Greek history, showing (above) the main per

place, the honour and glory of the ruler to the dignity and freedom of man. The Greeks in their cities consulted and voted, revered gods in man's image, developed philosophy and literature, perfected sculpture and architecture, enjoyed sacred tragedy and social comedy, played musical instruments and engaged in athletics.

In the fifth century B.C. this civilization was threatened by a full-scale invasion from the autocratic Empire of Persia, the first round in the classic struggle between Europe and Asia. United by the threat, the land power of Sparta and the sea power of Athens drove back, with greatly inferior forces, the biggest armada which the western world had yet seen. A golden age followed. But it was not to endure. The Greeks failed to preserve their unity, which broke down in a thirty years war between the two main states and their respective satellites: the militarist oligarchy or Sparta and the democracy of Athens, now infected by the taint of imperialism. It ended ignominiously in the defeat of Athens, with support from the former common enemy, Persia.

Unity was finally imposed on Greece by conquest only. In the fourth century the northern state of Macedonia, still a traditionalist monarchy, under Alexander the Great, conquered the other Greek states, whose democratic spirit was waning, then combined them to complete their initial defeat of the Persians, building up a Greek empire in Asia at Persian expense. Alexander made himself a Greek God, respected the Greek mind and character, preserved Greek institutions, shifted the centre of gravity from Europe to Asia, diffused Greek culture throughout a wider, more cosmopolitan world, but died too soon.

As disunity and disorder returned under his successors, the Romans, a nation of

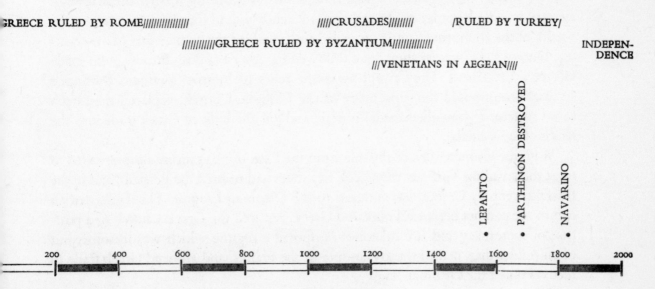

d influences, and (*below*) some of the events mentioned in this book.

soldiers, administrators and engineers, methodically took over the Greek world, completing in their own way the process which Alexander had begun. They imposed law and order, extorted taxes, maintained garrisons, appreciated Greek art and imitated it on a commercial scale, staged circuses and gladiatorial shows, built roads and baths and waterworks, reduced the Greek city states to municipalities and combined them at last, at the expense of Greek freedom, beneath a stable and unified system of government.

Roman rule declined under the pressure of tribes from without, and of a new religion, Christianity, from within. Christianity filled the vacuum created by the general decay of morality, the gulf between rich and poor, and the scepticism of the Greek philosophers, now discarding the heterogeneous pagan gods of their ancestors and seeking a new conception of divine unity in the One God. The Greeks responded eagerly to the new religion, finding in it a source of opposition to Roman authority, contributing their energy and their culture to the creation of the Orthodox Church and its establishment as the official religion in the East, and gaining a new lease of life for the Greek people under the Christian Empire of Byzantium.

The Byzantine Emperors were revered as divine, maintained an autocratic rule reinforced by a rigid central bureaucracy, built new cities, cathedrals and palaces, and evolved a new Greek Christian art, but eventually, in an excess of centralization, stifled the spirit of Greece itself, seizing its revenues, closing its schools, allowing its cities and roads to decay, and depriving of all effective power the municipal institutions which were the last survival of classical civilization.

From the sixth century A.D. Slav tribes from the North began to filter into Greece, occupying neglected agricultural lands, introducing a permanent foreign element into the population. In the eleventh century the Normans, tempted by the wealth of the Byzantine Empire, invaded and occupied the greater part of the country. During the Crusades they were followed by other Frankish princes, who made Greece a Latin land. They swept away the relics of Roman Law and Byzantine civilization, imposed the supremacy of the Catholic Church, replaced the Greek social structure by an alien feudal system, and put the bulk of Greek trade into the hands of the Venetians.

With the ultimate turn of the tide from the East, the Byzantine Empire failed to resist the invading Turks, as the Greek city states had resisted the Persians, and in the fifteenth century Greece was annexed to the Ottoman Empire. The Turks put an end to the conflict between Frank and Greek, restored the Greek Church to a position of supremacy and full toleration, imposed a regime which was irksome, but often milder than that of the Byzantines or the Franks, and allowed Greek trade to recover under the Ottoman flag.

As time went on Greek officials grew powerful at the Sultan's court, to the general benefit of their countrymen, while the Church became the active focus of a new Greek nationalism. Throughout the eighteenth century thoughts of independence grew, as the Greeks, responsive as ever to new ideas, reacted in turn to the British and French Revolutions. With the hope of raising a revolt, the Russians, posing as the champions of Greek Orthodox Christians, invaded the Peloponnese, but without success.

By the nineteenth century, with the decline of Turkish power, the revolt had become inevitable. It broke out in 1821. After some ten years of confused and venomous warfare, involving the final intervention of the Western Powers, Greece became, for the first time in its history, a united, independent state. Starting as a monarchy, first under a Bavarian, then under a Danish dynasty, it became a republic for a period after the First World War, but finally reverted to the monarchy which it retains today.

Such is the history of Greece and the Greeks. A vigorous, adventurous people, passionate in feeling and realistic in mind, they achieved at their best, by conscious effort, a rare degree of balance between the opposing forces of man's nature, rising to heights of achievement in life and art and politics which he has not since surpassed. The Greeks of today are a more mixed race, their stock diluted throughout the centuries with the foreign blood of emancipated slaves and invading Slavs. But they have inherited the spirit and character and tradition of classical Greece. Children still of their light and landscape, close to the earth which bore them and to the seas which carried them to wider horizons, they are a people for ever wide awake to life in all its aspects.

2

Crete and its heirs

The mountains of Crete sweep down to the sea with a bold dramatic air, each range echoing the other like a progression of rhythmic stanzas. Inland from the port of Heraklion, with its thickset weathered Venetian bastions, the rhythm is broken abruptly by a peak, jutting upwards and aside in free and insolent discord. It was here that Zeus died, and the peak describes his profile. Beneath it, in a landscape of bone-white limestone, yielding to stubble and vines and scattered groves of olives, lie the ruins of the city of Knossos. This, for seven hundred years, was the home of Minoan civilization.

It was here that Theseus came, from Athens, to slay the Minotaur, the monstrous creature, half bull, half man, which lived in King Minos's labyrinth. A sacrificial party of Athenian youths and maidens accompanied him, two of the 'maidens' being in fact effeminate youths whom he had disguised and coached as such. Ariadne, the daughter of the King and the sister of the Minotaur, fell in love with Theseus, and led him through the maze with a ball of thread to the monster's lodging, where he performed the deed. Emerging splashed with blood, he abducted Ariadne, stealing away by sea with his party. On his instructions the two effeminate youths had killed the guards of the women's quarters and rescued the maidens. Alternatively the Minotaur was simply a Cretan general called Taurus, a wrestler, who ran off with all the prizes at the games, until Theseus threw him three times and was given Ariadne as a reward. On his way home to Athens he abandoned her, on the island of Naxos.

These myths derive from the period when Knossos was known and respected by the rest of the Greek world as the centre of a powerful empire. It seems that, in about the fifteenth century B.C., the Athenians rebelled against a Cretan tyrant who had taken hostages from them – the youths and maidens of Theseus. Theseus, with a secretly built fleet, carried out a raid on Knossos, which he found undefended

FOUR THOUSAND YEARS AGO, the Palace of Minos, at Knossos, was the centre of a flourishing empire. Its charm today lies in its free and natural frescoes and reliefs: this sacred bull, head balefully bowed, feet pawing the ground, decorates the approach to the palace.

KNOSSOS HAS A DOMESTIC AIR, expert, intimate and comfortable. These vast jars, big enough to hide the forty thieves, were used to store oil and wine.

owing to the absence of the Cretan fleet in Sicily. He sacked the city, killed the King, and married his daughter Ariadne. He left her on Naxos, not far from Crete, owing to a local custom by which a woman lost her lands if she went overseas with her husband. The labyrinth may well have been the palace at Knossos, which was decorated everywhere with the *labrys*, or double-axe, the emblem of an Anatolian cult.

The excavations of Sir Arthur Evans, whose bust in bronze, with a slightly startled expression, sits perched on the top of a column by the entrance to the palace grounds, have helped to confirm both myth and history. Here is a labyrinth indeed, at several levels, of rooms and courtyards, corridors and staircases, in which Theseus and his friends might well have lost their way. Much reconstructed, the palace is solidly built from massive blocks of stone, while the principal halls and verandahs have colonnades of stout, round gypsum columns, red or black in colour.* In the Egypt of the Pharaohs the temple tended to overshadow the palace. In Crete, on the other hand, as in Anatolia, the palace and the temple were one. The lay and religious functions of the Minoan priest-kings were closely linked. A room, near the entrance, which resembles a bath, was in fact designed for the purpose of religious purification, by anointment with oil. The Throne Room, with its tall royal-episcopal seat, has been compared by Sir Arthur Evans to a consistory or a chapter-house, and has a similar sunken bath – a 'lustral area'. The maze of small rooms which adjoin it are essentially religious in character: they are shrines or crypts which were used for various ritual purposes. The houses and villas, surrounding the main palace, contain rooms of a similar nature.

But the general air of this vast rambling palace is more domestic than religious. The rooms themselves, with their unpretentious rectangular doorways, are not large. The corridors and stairways seem narrow. The impression is one of intimacy and comfort. Moreover the Minoans show here an aptitude for sanitary engineering unsurpassed either by the Egyptians before them or the Greeks after them. Their plumbing is remarkably up-to-date. There are signs of a system of running water, and an efficient network of gutters and drains and sewers, with conduit pipes so contrived as to prevent flooding and so tapered as to prevent stoppage. In the Queen's toilet room there is a water-closet, with a flushing arrangement and traces of a wooden seat, while in the room above there is a bath whose rim has apparent supports for a sponge rail. There is also an apparatus showing a distinct affinity to the *bidet*.

But the charm of Knossos lies in its interior decoration – in the frescoes which once covered the walls of its rooms, and of which fragments remain, imaginatively restored, both in the palace itself and in the museum of Heraklion. On a wall by the entrance to the palace is the relief, in plaster, of a handsome Minoan bull, head

* Plate, p. 25.

balefully bowed, feet pawing the ground in preparation for a charge.* Ritualistic as the origins of the Minoan paintings may be, they have a gay, free, natural quality, reflecting a delight in the decorative aspects of birds and beasts and fishes and flowers, together with a modish sophistication, suggesting at once the decadence of the 'nineties and the aesthetic impulses of the *art nouveau* period.

Among the animals partridges and bulls predominate – both initially objects of worship. Here a frieze of partridges, like the birds still fattened in cages by the proprietors of Cretan cafés, poses, together with a hoopoe, against a pattern of leaves and flowers devised in the manner of William Morris or William de Morgan. The labyrinth itself may derive from the partridges – from the brushwood maze, used to decoy the female to the cage of the male, and reproduced on a floor in mosaic to guide the performers in an imitative ritual dance. An elongated, elegant bull holds the stage in a circus painting, set in a *trompe-l'œil* frame. A slim black girl turns a somersault over its back, while a youth waits to catch her and another confronts it, holding its horns. These acrobatic sports of the bull-ring, religious in origin, were a feature of Minoan life, and captives, like the youths and maidens of Theseus, were trained to take part in them. In another fresco a blue monkey crouches to gather a saffron-yellow crocus, blooming like the tulips of later Turkish art.

The young ladies and gentlemen portrayed in the frescoes have a fashionable epicene air. Both sexes alike have slim boyish figures, long legs, narrow hips and wasp waists, and wear their hair in long curling tresses. The young prince in his brief pleated kilt and his grand plumed headdress might have stepped out of a ballet designed by Bakst. The three ringleted dancing girls in blue might have been drawn by Aubrey Beardsley. Admiring the *chic* of one of these young Minoan ladies, a French scholar christened her *La Parisienne*. But it was not only in painting that the Minoans excelled. Inspired initially by Egypt, but with a strong originality, they perfected sculptural arts and crafts of their own. In the museum are statuettes, vases, and seals, in stone and metal and wood, so finely carved and engraved, so alive with movement, as to furnish, here in the Crete of the seventeenth century B.C., a worthy ancestry for the fine arts of Renaissance Europe.

Knossos faces north, towards the islands and coasts of the Aegean. Phaestos, its contemporary rival, faces south, towards the coast of Libya. The road to it winds through a break in the mountains, up a bright white valley of flaring vines and smoking olives, then over the hills and down into an ample plain of burnished stubble. Here on a table-land of rock stands the acropolis of Phaestos, surveying to its north Mount Ida and to its east Mount Lassithi, rival birthplaces of Zeus, while to the south of it a satellite range, like a reflection of Ida, shelters its lands from the sea. The palace, smaller than that of Knossos, gains in grandeur from its commanding situation. Its bold, mortarless walls and stout square columns, its open courtyard

* Plate, p. 19.

spread at the feet of Mount Ida and looking down in its turn over a carpet of rice-fields, interwoven with a tapestry of olives, have a dignity worthy of the sacred peak, hovering in snow-capped seclusion above. Its rooms are small, but its corridors are spacious, its stairways broad and shallow. The broadest ends in a wall; for it is a flight of theatre seats. At Knossos there are two such flights, set at right angles. Here is the forerunner of the familiar Greek theatre, whose seats were set in a semicircle.

Theseus, Ariadne and the Minotaur survive, in arts and crafts, in a number of tourist shops within the Venetian ramparts of Heraklion. As befitted an island in a key commercial position, Crete remained in the hands of the Venetians for nearly five hundred years, and only fell to the Turks late in the seventeenth century with the final surrender of the port, the Venetian Candia, after a twenty-four-year siege. It still contains the façades of a few Venetian houses, and a handsome Italian Renaissance fountain, placed there by its final defender Morosini, the great Venetian admiral, who later succeeded for a while in reoccupying the Peloponnese, and even Athens itself. Crete did not free itself from the Turks until the end of the nineteenth century; thus until lately Heraklion was still primarily Turkish in character, with ramshackle bazaars and colour-washed houses in a labyrinth of winding lanes and courtyards. These still survive, but in the last world war the town as a whole was severely damaged, and it is now bettering itself, in a nondescript modern style. In a new city centre is a neon-lit square, where the Cretan bourgeoisie relaxes, beneath eucalyptus trees, to the sound of loud loud-speakers, watched in the evenings by an eternal parade of Cretan youth, pacing restlessly to and fro. They are a dour people, more silent than the Greeks of the mainland, but as courageous in spirit and as stoutly independent in outlook.

Retimo, spared by the war and by progress, has retained its Turkish atmosphere, and even its Turkish minarets, rising like chimneys above narrow streets with sagging, bow-fronted balconies. The road to it runs out along the coast from Heraklion, crosses white river beds blushing pink with oleanders, then winds up and down over the northern spurs of the Ida range. Here is a sunlit landscape, sharply in focus. A small, domed chapel gleams white on a hilltop. The surrounding rock forms, bold and blue, contrast with the threaded texture of vine and olive and cypress, in brilliant clashing greens. Here in this landscape is the village where El Greco was born. Here is another village where women sit rocking, not babies in cradles, but sucking-pigs on spits, to tempt the hungry traveller. Inland there winds a fruitful valley, where the limbs of the olive trees twist and twirl, as though in a dance, on the dry white earth, the young saplings parting from the parent trunk to gather around it, dancing too.

High at the head of the valley, amid ancient, spreading oak trees, stands the weatherbeaten monastery of Arkadi. A fortress of the Faith throughout the centuries, with an Italianate Baroque church façade, its walls are still pitted and scarred, and its chapel still roofless, from a Turkish bombardment of 1866, when its Abbot, and five hundred villagers and monks, preferred martyrdom to surrender, and set a light to the powder magazine. A later Abbot, during the Second World War, armed it as a secret centre of resistance against the Germans. Weapons and ikons hang together on the monastery walls, with faded photographs of monkish warriors, and blackened paintings of heroic scenes in the never-forgotten Greek War of Independence.

Above Retimo tower the remote White Mountains, their peaks a sunlit pink after the winter snows; their grey flanks powdered with golden grasses, or thatched with green arbutus; their villages perched high around mountain springs, beneath the shade of plane trees, where a few orchards and terraces of thin soil have been wrung from the menacing, stony ground. Here the warriors of Crete swagger around in moustachios, top-boots, black shirts and spectacular black-and-tan breeches, recalling and still secretly hankering for the days when they resisted the Germans, harbouring British officers in mountain caves, and the days before that when they resisted the Turks. Now there is no one to resist, poverty is with them still, and peace seems flat. But there is always the blood feud, village against village, family against family. The heirs of Minos are a vigorous race, not easily tamed.

Mycenae and the Heroic Age

The seaward approach to Mycenae from Crete is through Nauplia, a fortified Venetian harbour, more imposing than Heraklion, at the head of the Argolid Gulf. It was here that Morosini died, after his invasion of the Peloponnese. The Venetians were masters of military architecture, and the citadel of Nauplia – the Naples of Romania* – commanding a small Greek town, is a bold and streamlined fortress, with a zigzag stairway, a sweeping aqueduct, and incisive functional battlements. Today the buildings within its ramparts, once used by the Turks as a prison, are abandoned. One of its cells, in common with others in countless Peloponnesian castles, is said to have been inhabited by Kolokotrones, the bandit leader of the War of Independence. On a wall is scrawled an inscription in Greek, by some later prisoner. 'In prison', he has written, 'the four monsters possessed me: Desire, Self-pity, Introspection and Despair.' After the War of Independence Nauplia was for five years the seat of the new Greek Government. On an islet offshore, commanding the harbour and once joined to it by a breakwater, stands a miniature Venetian stronghold, as compact and complete in every detail as a child's toy fort. The

* The name applied by the West to the Byzantine Empire.

COLONNADES OF GYPSUM COLUMNS, in vivid red and black, support the principal halls of Knossos. This is the entrance to the Hall of the Double Axes, so called from the masons' marks in the great stone blocks of the walls.

THE LION GATE OF MYCENAE. The entrance through the massive walls of the city is crowned by a relief of two lions, lithe and slender, with a sacred pillar between them. Only their heads, perhaps of gilded bronze, have gone.

Greeks once used it as a home for retired executioners, whom they did not like having around. They now use it, perhaps for a similar reason, as a hotel for the richer foreign tourists.

Inland from Nauplia, the fertile plain of Argos spreads up to the feet of its guardian mountain ranges. Homer called it 'horse-feeding Argos', because of its reputation as a breeding place for horses. The city of Argos was one of the earliest in Greece. It was eclipsed by Mycenae, but revived after a few centuries, and eventually destroyed its rival. After the Dorian invasions, Argos became a rival of Sparta for the domination of the Peloponnese, and for many centuries an important factor in the balance of power between the various Greek states. Little of interest remains of the city today but some dozen tiers of its theatre seats, climbing the steep lower slopes of a fortified mountain which rises in isolation from the plain.

Mycenae commands its northern outlet, where the road, in the past a vital trade route, runs through a narrow pass towards the Gulf of Corinth and so to the lands of Northern Greece. It must have enabled Mycenae to control Corinth. From the head of a gorge, with an impenetrable grey-gold cliff behind it, the city, bound by its massive cyclopean walls, looks down over a twisting terraced hillside to the deep red earth and the rich green crops of the Argive plain below. A product of the Heroic, Homeric Age of Greece, it was not yet a city in the later Hellenic sense, but rather a palace-fortress, relatively small, the seat of a central government, dominating a quantity of townships and villages around it and maintaining a wide sphere of influence, with subordinate strongholds farther afield. Its red-grey walls, from ten to fifty feet thick, are built from rough-hewn slabs of stone, rectangular or polygonal, each fitting into the other with a precision scorning mortar. Its gateway of three stout monoliths rises, crowned in heraldic style with a relief of two lions, lithe and slender, their necks stretching upwards, their forepaws resting on an altar, with a sacred pillar, between them – the symbol of strength and protection. Only their heads, made separately, perhaps of gilded bronze, have gone. The lions may be the emblems of a cult, inherited, like those of Crete, from Anatolia: they were the sacred attendants of Rhea, the mother-goddess of Phrygia, whence the ruling dynasty of Pelops was said to have sprung.

A royal road, broad enough for chariots – the principal means of road travel, apart from the mule, in Mycenean times – leads up to the palace, which was built at the highest point of the citadel. Its rooms were less open than those of Knossos with their verandahs and courtyards, perhaps because it was more of a fortress, perhaps because the climate of the Peloponnese was colder than that of Crete. But, as their surviving foundations show, they were large and well-situated, with spacious views over the plain beneath; and like the Cretan palaces which this had supplanted, they were well-endowed with frescoes.

It may well have been in one of these rooms that Agamemnon, King of Mycenae, was murdered by Aegisthus, who had previously murdered his father
Atreus, on his return from the siege of Troy. He was struck down, as Homer wrote,
at table, 'like an ox at the manger'; or, as Aeschylus preferred, in the bath, with a
net over his head; in any event finished off by Clytemnestra, with the axe which was
the emblem of Minoan, and now of Mycenean sovereignty. By Clytemnestra's
orders a watchman had been squatting on the roof of the palace for a year, watching
for the first spark of a beacon on a far-off peak, the last link in a chain of fires started
on Mount Ida, to announce the fall of Troy. The myth may have been derived from
a palace revolution of the twelfth century B.C., arising from local dynastic rivalries.
The name of Agamemnon, meaning 'very resolute', may have been a generic and
divine one, borne *ex officio*, as Zeus Agamemnon, by the Mycenean Kings. It was not
long after this period that the power of Mycenae, weakened perhaps by the Trojan
War, began to decline, under pressure from the invading Dorians.

Its earlier Kings were buried in shaft-graves, in the heart of the city within the
Lion Gate. Their cemetery makes a sacred enclosure, an elliptical compound, encircled by a double wall of slabs like large flat tombstones. As the period of settlement gave place, in the fifteenth century, to a period of expansion, their burial
habits changed. They built, outside the city walls, underground tombs like huge
domed beehives, architectural achievements as striking in their way as the pyramids
of Egypt. Two of these, known as the tomb of Clytemnestra, and the Treasury of
Atreus or the tomb of Agamemnon, survive intact. In each a high broad passage,
between monumental walls, leads to a doorway some twenty feet high. The lintel
block of the Treasury of Atreus weighs a hundred and ten tons. Inside, there rises,
to a height of fifty feet, a great circular hall, symbolic perhaps of the lower world,
its walls sloping gradually upwards to end in a dome of conical shape. This was the
outer sepulchre, for members of the family. The King himself was buried in a
smaller inner chamber, leading out of it. The bodies were surrounded by a number
of valuables, which were often removed as time went on – a characteristic element
in the cult of the dead.

Schliemann, the German archaeologist, who came to Mycenae, in the steps of
Agamemnon, from the field of Troy, found in the tombs a treasure store of golden
ornaments, products of the age when the art of Mycenae was flowering into a baroque refinement of its own. There was jewellery of all kinds, pins and brooches,
combs and fillets, bracelets and belts and buttons, all carved with the effigies of
lions and eagles, doves and griffins, butterflies and dragons and octopi. There were
signet rings, their *intaglios* delicately engraved with heroic scenes of battle; goblets
as finely chased as the works of the Italian Renaissance; embossed swords and
breast-plates and two-headed axes; even gold leaves, strewn around the dead,

among unopened oysters, left for them to eat. The gold was usually soldered with borax, as it is by jewellers today. Most dramatic of all were the golden portrait masks, each placed over the face of a corpse and clearly depicting its features – which were often distinctly Hellenic. The Egyptians instead used wooden masks, and made no attempt at portraiture.

Of one of his rarest finds, a dragon-headed handle, Schliemann writes: 'If Homer had seen this extraordinary handle when it was entire, he would undoubtedly have ascribed it to the skilful hand of Hephaestus, and would have uttered his sense of beauty in the words ... "a wonder to look upon".'

As Schliemann worked on the site, 'for the first time since its capture by Argives in 468 B.C., and so for the first time during 2,344 years, the Acropolis of Mycenae has a garrison, whose watch fires seen by night throughout the whole plain of Argos carry back the mind to the watch kept for Agamemnon's return from Troy, and the signal which warned Clytemnestra and her paramour of his approach. But this time the object of the occupation by soldiers is of a more peaceful character, for it is merely intended to inspire awe among the country people, and to prevent them from making clandestine excavations in the tombs, or approaching them while we are working in them.' One day the news of a sensational discovery 'spread like wild fire through the Argolid and people came by thousands from Argos, Nauplia and the villages to see the wonder.' It was the body of a man of the Heroic Age, still in reasonably good condition. 'The round face, with all its flesh, had been wonderfully preserved under its ponderous golden mask; there was no vestige of hair, but both eyes were perfectly visible, also the mouth which, owing to the enormous weight that had pressed upon it, was wide open and showed thirty-two beautiful teeth.' The body, which might have crumbled immediately, held out for two days, when a druggist from Argos pickled it in alcohol and so preserved it.

Chief among Mycenae's satellite strongholds was Tiryns, which lies between Argos and the sea. It is a rough-walled city which stands on a mound, its walls built, according to legend, by the Cyclops themselves, who were masons from Asia Minor. To subsequent ages they appeared to be the work of giants; hence it was natural to assume that Hercules himself had lived within them. His twelve labours were performed for the King of Mycenae and, as the Sun God, he must have had a hand in draining the marshes, which once surrounded the city. Tiryns today is a confused mass of masonry, from which the archaeologist is able to disentangle two palaces, a small and a large, their rooms including separate quarters for the King and Queen, with no communication between them, store-rooms built within the thickness of the walls, and a bathroom whose floor was a single gigantic slab. An impressive amenity is a well-built subway, leading out beneath the ramparts, its vast stones rising to form a pointed vault, without apparent support. A similar passage leads down into the depths of the rock at Mycenae, where a cistern was built to hold a reserve supply of water, in the event of a siege. Both reflect a style of architecture familiar in the buildings of the Hittites in Asia Minor.

Tiryns, like Mycenae, was destroyed by the Dorians, and Argos reigned supreme once more. The Heroic, Homeric Age was to give way to a new Greek civilization.

3

Sparta, the 'wise and practised warrior'

Mountains form an unbroken western barrier to the Argolid plain and gulf. The road winds up over them, looking back at every turn to the sea, then forsakes it, running straight across fertile uplands, among poplars and mulberries and waving wheat, towards Tripolis, the capital of Arcadia. From here another road runs southward, winding gradually down over green hillsides into the broad red valley of the Eurotas. In this 'sown land' of Laconia, spread like a carpet between the lofty walls of Mount Parnon on the one hand and Mount Taygetus on the other, lies Sparta. The Dorians, Greeks maybe from the north, founded Sparta – conquerors already of the greater part of the Peloponnese, destroyers of Tiryns and Mycenae and of the relics of the civilization of the ancient Heroic Age. A race of landsmen and soldiers, with a large population and a fertile soil, the Spartans soon, in the words of Herodotus, 'shot up and flourished like a sturdy tree', becoming the strongest power in Greece at a time when no naval power, as Crete had been and as Athens and Phoenicia were to become, existed to threaten their supremacy.

Mythically, since Greeks must be descended from Gods, they were at pains to trace their ancestry back to Hercules, and at the same time to the Cretan and Mycenean dynasties, which they now supplanted. Racially, they kept their stock pure, excluding the foreigner, refraining from intermarriage with the conquered inhabitants, imposing their own way of life upon them, and treating them as a subject race. Since this involved ruling over an active majority, the Spartans had to build up a strong militarist state; and this indeed suited their national bent. Sparta, as Plutarch put it, was more 'a wise and practised warrior' than a city.

31

As time went on, all was subordinated to the arts of war. The softening influences of home life were discouraged, and the Spartans, whatever their wealth and social position, were obliged to eat in 'messes', on rations fixed by the State. Their menus were frugal, their greatest delicacy a form of black broth, which was not considered appetizing abroad. When a certain King of Pontus expressed his dislike for it, his Spartan cook explained that 'those who eat this broth must first bathe in the Eurotas'. Luxury in Sparta was sternly eliminated. Commerce, hence wealth, was discouraged, since it involved intercourse with the foreigner. Spartan money was not generally current in Greece since it was made, deliberately, not of silver and gold but of iron, 'of great size and weight', so that a sum equivalent to a mere £50 'required a great room for its stowage and a yoke of oxen to draw it'. Clothes were simple, furniture utilitarian and functional. Land was divided up into equal portions. Within a constitution which was in theory a dual monarchy, with democratic safeguards, but in effect an oligarchy, Sparta became an egalitarian society, with a strong flavour of national socialism as we know it, secret police and all.

Morality was strict. Adultery was a crime – unless indeed it was condoned by the husband, for the purposes of breeding healthy stock. To fit them for childbirth, girls led a hardy, athletic life, running, wrestling and hurling javelins. Children, washed at birth in wine, instead of water, to test their strength, were dedicated to the State. If a child was unhealthy the authorities exposed it to die in a chasm on the slopes of Mount Taygetus; if it was healthy they returned it to its parents, until the age of seven. Then the boy was removed to lead a stern communal life, receiving a state education which taught him not merely to read and to write, but to play games, submit to discipline, endure hardships, and fight. At the age of twelve he discarded his tunic and was given a single garment, to wear throughout the year.

The boys 'were necessarily dirty, as they had no warm baths and ointments, except on certain days as a luxury. They slept all together in troops and companies, on beds of rushes which they themselves had picked on the banks of the Eurotas'. They were supervised by bigger boys, 'prefects', for whom they fagged, cooking their meals, carrying logs for them, and bringing them the food which, having little to eat, they were encouraged to steal from the gardens and from the messes of the older men, as a test of enterprise, being flogged or starved if they were caught. They took stealing so seriously that one, rather than reveal a fox's cub which he had hidden beneath his cloak, allowed it to tear out his entrails until he died. But they learnt also to use their brains: to give a good answer to a question, to talk briefly and pithily, in what came to be known as 'Laconic' style, and to recite poems and sing songs of a rousing patriotic nature. This way of life, that of the camp rather than the city, persisted until manhood. Its originator, Lycurgus, 'trained his countrymen neither to wish nor to understand how to live as private men, but, like bees, to be parts of the commonwealth, and gather round their chief, forgetting themselves in their enthusiastic patriotism, and utterly devoted to their country'.

As Thucydides wrote, prophetically: 'Suppose ... that the city of Sparta were to become deserted and that only the temples and foundations of buildings remained, I think that future generations would, as the time passed, find it very difficult to believe that the place had really been as powerful as it was represented to be.' For, unlike Athens, which he thought would appear to us more powerful than in fact it was, Sparta boasted no great temples or monuments, but was more a collection of villages than a city. Thus today, in fact, little remains to be seen of it.

The modern city is built on a new site. Designed under the auspices of Otho, the first King of Greece, not long after the War of Independence, it is an inconsiderable country town, but boldly and imaginatively planned. It consists of a single double boulevard and a great broad square, its colour-washed houses confined to a single storey, so as to afford the Greeks in its cafés an uninterrupted view of the majestic snow-capped skyline of Taygetus, towering above its roofs. Palms and oleanders bloom in its streets, roses rampage over its gardens, giving it an air of scented ease, while the Spartans, unlike their sterner forbears, recline by the hour in comfortable barbers' chairs, discussing Spartan affairs to the song of caged canaries.

The churches of Mistra

The very name of Sparta was gradually forgotten during the Byzantine period, and remained so until King Otho revived it. The medieval city was built, on yet another site, on a spur of Mount Taygetus. Its name was Mistra. By this time the Slavs, filtering down from the north, had overrun the Peloponnese to such an extent that travellers referred to it as 'the Sclavonian land'. They occupied not only the slopes of the mountain but the rich valley of the Eurotas, and it was to hold them in check, cutting them off from these resources, that the Frankish prince, William de Villehardouin, founded Mistra, a powerful walled stronghold with a castle commanding the plain. When the Greeks revolted against the Franks it became, and remained, a flourishing Byzantine city, under a line of semi-independent despots. Though it declined under the Turks, it was abandoned only in the nineteenth century, when its inhabitants moved to modern Sparta.

In essence it is a Byzantine city still, for all its ruined aspect. Up its steep hillside the domes of churches arise, above the debris of narrow winding streets. Their red-tiled corrugated roofs radiate striking patterns, bold in light and shadow; their stone walls are weathered and warmed by the sun, patterned too with dog-toothed and herringboned courses of brick. Above, the walls of the Frankish castle still ride the skyline, looking down on the vaulted halls of a spacious Byzantine palace.

Beneath, the plain stretches away from the shingle bed of the winding Eurotas, green with mulberries and cypresses, slender as chimneys above a glow of red roofs and a smoking mist of olives.*

The churches of Mistra gather around three Byzantine monasteries, of which two still thrive as such. All are painted within, in a style which reflects the flowering of late Byzantine art – that of the second Renaissance which followed the Iconoclast age, and which has been compared in its quality, though not in its character, to the contemporary work of the *Quattrocento* in Italy. Essentially Greek, it was inspired by the East rather than the West, and indeed was itself to inspire the West, through the art of El Greco and others.

Two schools of painters, the Macedonian and the Cretan, have enriched the innumerable varied surfaces of the walls and domes of Mistra. Glowing darkly, materializing slowly in the twilit obscurity of the vaulted churches, the murals, now in earthy browns and blues and reds, now lightening into sophisticated pinks and greens, represent, as it were, the slow coming to life, in human terms, of the more stylized figures, the Christ and Virgin, angels and evangelists and prophets of the earlier Byzantine painters. Here, for all the solemnity of subject and formality of treatment, the familiar scenes in the life of Christ and His Saints have a new air of intimacy, a delight in life for its own sake. Meanwhile time and the elements have left their own weird mark, slashing harshly into the pictures with abstract patterns of mould, stained plaster and rough protruding brick.

Venetian ruins of Monemvasia

Three prongs, 'desert promontories', jut out into the sea from the Peloponnesian mountain mass. From the vale of the Eurotas, basking in fruitfulness, a rough road winds over the easterly prong, through a hot drying country of rocks and whins and straggling olives, where mere slivers of corn-land survive. It is a dying land, with a dwindling population. At the end of the road, as at the end of the world, a sudden hump-backed rock juts up from a sea gleaming as still as a sheet of ground glass. Here, forgotten, is the outpost of Monemvasia. Once, it seems, a naval station of the Minoans, it became in Byzantine times a place of refuge from the Slavs, and grew into a notable commercial city of the Eastern Mediterranean – the Greek equivalent of what Venice later became. The Venetians themselves took it over from the Greeks and, thanks to its impregnable position, were able to hold it against the Turks, for some time after the rest of the Peloponnese had fallen into their hands. They called the place Napoli di Malvasia, and made from its grapes the noted Malmsey wine.

No wine grows in Monemvasia today. Only a small modern village, on the mainland, clusters around an unfrequented harbour. The rock itself, once as proud

* Plate, p. 36.

IN THE HEART OF ARCADIA, the medieval Frankish castle of Karitaina juts out above the village like the prow of a ship, breasting the rough rocks tumbling around it. The castle was built to keep both Slavs and Greeks at bay.

as Gibraltar, is now all but abandoned. Crowned by a walled Byzantine citadel, it drops headlong to the sea, red as a raw side of meat with veins of grey, then black as though scorched as it shelves into the turquoise water. Built precariously on a shelf, by the brink of the sea, is a village, now almost deserted, whose half-dozen churches, Greek and Latin, recall the centuries when it was a thriving town.

A single tavern, vaulted and cool beneath the blazing towering rock, now caters for the traveller with such sparse fresh fish as may come its way, its walls hung with faded classical prints, its tables strewn unexpectedly with tattered Victorian novels, including an early work by the author of *Vice Versa*. Dizzily perched above, within the walls of the citadel, is a domed and buttressed church of the thirteenth century. Over all there reigns an uncanny stillness, as of a place which no longer exists. The end of a continent, it reflects also the end of an epoch of history. Even the kestrels, hovering above the crags, seem suspended in a motionless trance.

The central prong of the Peloponnese thrusts sharply down from the snow-capped range of Mount Taygetus. Taygetus, more than Parnon, seems to wall off Sparta from the rest of the world. It rises in layers, one above the other, a sheer eight thousand feet from the plain. The spine of the mountain sprawls across the skyline like that of a four-humped dragon, its tail curling away to the north; its ribs are streaked with snow, like the flanks of a tiger.

Within the recesses of the mountain the Minyae lived. Descendants of the Argo-nauts, they were given grants of land by the Spartans, with whom they inter-married. But it was not long, according to Herodotus, before they 'began to go too far, even claiming a share in the royal power, and doing other things no less im-proper'. The Spartans arrested them, but they evaded execution by escaping from the prison, dressed in the clothes of their wives, who had come to bid them farewell. Thus they remained for a while on Taygetus, but finally agreed to go quietly. Their name may well have descended to the Mainates, a surviving Greek enclave among the Slavs of Taygetus, so remote in their fastnesses that they escaped conversion to Christianity until as late as the ninth century A.D. Later they were a thorn in the side both of Crusaders and Turks.

The mountain flings out two guardian heights, and the road winds up between them, through the glen maybe where the Spartans exposed their children. It is a dramatic ascent, through forests of cypress and pine, between jagged grey rocks which career away down to the dry bed of a stream below. Presently the snows seep down, melting into trickles of water, and the high slopes emerge, grey as an ele-phant's hide, above pastures pink with flowers. Beyond the watershed the descent, from Laconia into Messenia, is less abrupt. The road follows the lip of a narrow gorge of cavernous grey-gold limestone, then winds away down, through woods of sweet chestnut, between terraced fields, to a plain cloudy with olives and, once again, the sea.

CLASSICAL SIMPLICITY AND BYZANTINE RICHNESS: the temple of Apollo at Bassae, a gem of Greek architecture, is worlds away from the monastery church of Mistra.

'Good to plant and good to ear', the Messenian plain is even more fruitful than the vale of the Eurotas, and as such excited the covetous designs of the warlike, land-grabbing Spartans. Coming as conquerors rather than colonists, they laid up for themselves here a perennial source of revolt, which in the long run sapped their strength. Today the fruitfulness brings wealth to Kalamata, the largest port in the southern Peloponnese, which is famed for its olives. Appropriately, its sea-front, otherwise sultry and bleak, is shaded by an alley of pleached and pollarded olive trees. Its castle walls recall William de Villehardouin, the Crusading Prince of Achaia and founder of Mistra, who was born within them; its river banks the first service of thanksgiving, sung by twenty-four priests and five thousand armed soldiers, to celebrate the first victory of the Greek Revolution.

Inland from Kalamata, standing alone, is the peak of Ithome, called after one of the nymphs who nursed Zeus. Here was the guerrilla stronghold, where the Messenians held out so obstinately that the Spartans were finally reduced to calling the Athenians to their aid. They soon regretted this, mistrusting the unorthodox and adventurous spirit of the Athenians and fearing that they would side with the rebels, so sent them home, thus causing the first breach between Athens and Sparta which finally led to the Peloponnesian War. When the rebels finally surrendered and were exiled from the Peloponnese, the Athenians gave them a home at Navpaktos, their naval station on the Gulf of Corinth. It was the Thebans, during their brief period of supremacy in Greece, who eventually restored them to their homes, assisted by a rising of Messenian slaves.

Epaminondas the Theban, after his victory against Sparta at Mantinea, founded for them the city of Messene, on the slopes of the mountain, as one of a ring of fortresses designed to keep Sparta in check. Pausanias was impressed by the strength of the city walls, implying that they were comparable to those of Babylon. Though partly in ruins they look formidable still, running down the slopes of the mountain to an imposing double gateway, between towers, and a circular chamber within it. They are built from massive slabs of stone, well moulded and finished, with their surfaces rusticated as in buildings of the Italian Renaissance.

To the west the Peloponnese runs away in an undulating landscape, green with vines and pink with wild flowers, to one of the world's most striking natural harbours, the classical Pylos, the Byzantine Navarino. The wide arc of its bay is protected from the ocean by a long wall of rock, resembling a promontory but in fact an island. To the north a narrow channel divides it from the mainland. To the south it throws out further walls, pierced only here and there to make natural harbour gates. In this enclosed space, at an interval of some two thousand years, were fought two of history's crucial naval engagements.

The first was the Battle of Pylos, in the fifth century B.C., a dramatic victory of

the Athenians against the Spartans in the Peloponnesian War. The Athenians had
landed on the island and fortified it, using the rebellious Messenians as a garrison;
the Spartans tried to dislodge them. It was, as Thucydides remarks, a strange para-
dox 'for Athenians to be fighting a battle on land – and Spartan land too – against
Spartans attacking from the sea ... for at this time Sparta chiefly prided herself on
being a land power with an unrivalled army, and Athens on being a sea power with
the greatest navy in existence'. The battle turned out even more paradoxically.
After the Spartans had made a landing on the island, the Athenians, sailing in at both
entrances to the harbour, found themselves 'fighting an infantry battle from their
ships' as they boarded and captured those of the Spartans; meanwhile the shore-
bound Spartans, frantically wading into the sea in their armour to save their ships,
were 'fighting a sea battle on land'.

Sparta, besieged on the island, sued for peace; Athens rejected it; but the siege
dragged on. Cleon, the Athenian demagogue, a leather merchant and a product of
the new bourgeois democracy, blamed the generals and boasted that he could do
better. His bluff was called and, to the delight of his enemies, he was sent to try.
To their discomfiture, and to the astonishment of all, he succeeded, returning in
triumph to Athens with a number of high-ranking Spartan prisoners. Eventually
the Spartans made peace, and the first round in the Peloponnesian War went to the
Athenians.

The second great battle was that of Navarino, in the nineteenth century A.D.,
when Ibrahim Pasha, with his army of Egyptians, was harrying the Greeks as the
Athenians had harried the Spartans. An Allied fleet of British, French and Russians
sailed into the harbour, intending merely to make a show of force, but became involved in an action, and virtually annihilated the Turkish navy. The result was to
secure the independence of Greece, and permanently to weaken Turkey against the
threat from Russia. The holocaust is recalled by a marble obelisk, erected in 1927
as a memorial to the Allied admirals. It stands in the elegant arcaded square, which
was built by French troops after the battle. Commanding the bay, from a headland,
is a Venetian castle, used by the Turks as a prison, and a Greek Orthodox church,
its walls glowing a deep burnt orange against the blue sea shimmering below.

The heart of Arcadia

While wars and revolutions raged through the Peloponnese, the classical land of
Arcadia, to the north of Messenia, lived in peace. Its people claimed to have sprung
from the earth and to be older than the moon. Its landscape rolls away gently between the mountain ranges, less emphatic, less ordered than that of the southern
plains and valleys, with a haphazard quality all its own, and a deep serene fertility.

The rows of olives disappear; the fields are shaded by spreading oak trees, fresh green planes and chestnuts.

In medieval times the Arcadian peace was disturbed by the occupation of the Franks, who crowned the strategic hilltops with castles. Among them were Mate-grifon or 'Stop-Greek', and Karitaina, built to keep both Slavs and Greeks at bay. Karitaina, commanding the upper waters of the Alpheos, and thus the roads from the centre of the Peloponnese down to the western coastal plains, juts out from its peak like the prow of a ship, breasting the rough rocks tumbling around it.* A vil-lage clings to the slopes beneath it – a market for mules, wearing bright coloured saddle-cloths woven with vivid designs. Cypresses, alive with fluttering kestrels, rise like sentinels above the domes and roofs of two Byzantine churches. In one of them time has worn the murals away, leaving an abstract pattern of reds and browns, enlivened by jagged streaks of plaster.

Beneath the village the waters of the Alpheos run through a deep narrow gorge crossed by a handsome Venetian bridge. Beyond it, the road winds up over the opposite hillside to the remote mountain village of Andritsaina. Isolated from the world, it is a village in a stage-set, streets careering uphill in a crazy perspective, houses, rickety as dolls' houses, jostling and bulging around a cobbled square, where a fountain gushes surprisingly from the trunk of a mammoth plane tree. It is a stage-set bursting with sound and life, ringing and echoing, in the resonant mountain air, with the gabble of Greek voices, the braying of livestock, the splashing of mountain streams. A rough human rabble, eyes narrow with rapacity and alight with curios-ity, mobs the traveller, clamouring to provide him with mules and an escort to the Temple of Bassae. It is a village impoverished by war, whose inhabitants lost their cattle, and so their means of livelihood, to the Communists, and now seek to emi-grate to Australia and other lands overseas.

Above Andritsaina the road comes to an end; only a path winds on over the ridge, into a world remoter still. Here is the heart of Arcadia, the true Greek land-scape, at once rugged and gentle, moreover brimming with a light which is almost incandescent, a jewelled radiance which rarefies each stone, each leaf, each ripple on the face of the stream. The path follows its banks, through a lattice of plane trees; pauses by a spring where the trunk of a veteran tree has supplied a trough for the cool sweet waters; winds above it across pastures sweet with wild flowers, bright with the filigree of unfolding bracken and the clean lace embroidery of cow parsley; skirts the side of a mountain through woods of oak trees, their branches oddly lop-ped for timber, but still spreading shade over the dry red earth. It is a landscape ten-anted only by the Arcadian goat-herd, his goats of an aristocratic demeanour, with fine heraldic horns; a landscape silent but for the voice of the nightingale, singing all the day through, and for the dissonant Byzantine cadences of the goat bells

* Plate, p. 35.

THE SUNLIT GREEK LANDSCAPE inspires a pagan joy in colour, as in this village church of Moulki, on Salamis, with its domes washed pink against the rough blue-white walls.

THE PARTHENON, in serene isolation, raises its columns and pediments to the sky from the summit of the Acropolis. This is the west front, through the columns of the Propylae.

drifting up from the valley below. Higher and higher the path climbs, up and out beyond the trees into upper pastures, green amid the eroded outcrops of a blue-grey limestone. All of a sudden there arise, as though created by nature, growing from the rock and likewise pitted with erosion and coated with lichen, the blue-grey fluted columns of the Doric temple of Bassae.*

Standing here in solitude, the southern mountains of the Peloponnese falling away in blue layers around it, the temple unites in classic terms the grandeur of Greek landscape with the austerity of Greek architecture. Dedicated to Apollo, in his capacity as God of Health, it is said by Pausanias to have been built by the people of Phygalia, below, in gratitude for their delivery from plague; but it probably succeeded an earlier shrine on this high salubrious site. Built in the fifth century, it was the work of Ictinos, the architect of the Parthenon, which is some years earlier in date. Pausanias puts it first of all the temples of the Peloponnese, except that at Tegea, 'for the beauty of the stone and the neatness of the structure'. It hardly emulates the Parthenon, being smaller in proportion, narrower and more severely Doric in design, moreover built not of marble but of the humbler limestone of its natural setting.

In this setting, however, lies the essence of the Greek religion, with its worship of the earth and the heavens and all that is beautiful in nature; while in the temple itself lies the essence of Greek architecture, with all its logical simplicity of line and form. The Dorian warriors had emerged from the Dark Age as a race also of artists. They were to give to the Greek world an art, inherently masculine in conception, like nothing the world had seen before.

* Plate, p. 36.

4

Athens looks to the sea

Unlike Sparta, within its land-locked strongholds, Athens lies wide open to the sea. It faces the world across the radiant expanse of the blue Saronic Gulf, framed in a generous amphitheatre of coasts and islands and mountain ridges receding layer upon layer, in deepening blues, then falling out of sight into satellite gulfs, around it. Here, for thousands of years, have come the ships of all peoples. Here they come to-day, their tempo quickening, as though in a regatta, as they spank over the waves in the morning swell and the glittering morning light. Big ships race one another to the harbour, the Aegean sea foam licking boisterously at their haunches. Smaller Greek boats from the islands, scorning a pilot, overtake them, passengers crowding to the decks and waving and cheering, while the people on shore wave too.

Just so must Greeks have watched and waved and cheered at the Battle of Salamis. Athens evacuated, the Acropolis fallen, they crowded the shores of the island of Salamis, while the battle raged in the narrows before them, Persian and Greek ships ramming and grappling with one another in a pandemonium of din and confusion. Xerxes himself watched from the mainland opposite, seated on a golden throne beneath a golden umbrella, and surrounded by reporters whose duty it was to record the battle. They had to record a defeat. Themistocles, the Athenian admiral, having chosen the place of battle, which would hamper a large fleet, now chose the time of it, awaiting the morning swell, which would hamper high-sterned ships. 'Pray to the winds,' said the Delphic oracle, 'for they will fight stoutly on the side of Greece.' Victory was sealed by the subsequent land battle of Plataea. Thus democracy was saved, the imperialist foiled in his boast that he would 'pass through Europe from end to end and make it one country, so that the sun will not look down upon any land beyond the boundaries that are ours'.

It was a democracy rooted in the sea, in the growth of a mercantile class, competing with the nobility, and a class of sailors, the 'nautical rabble' of Aristotle, claiming ultimate political recognition in the state whose wealth they had helped to amass. Themistocles it was who first converted this seafaring spirit into a military asset. He saw that Athens could never hold her own as a land power, and made her a sea power, building her a fleet for use ostensibly against the neighbouring island of Aegina, but actually, as he foresaw, against Persia. As Pericles afterwards put it, 'We must try to think of ourselves as islanders.' In the words of Plato, he made the Athenians roving sailors instead of stationary soldiers; in the words of his opponents, he took away from them the shield and the spear and reduced them to the oar and the rower's bench.

It took time to convert the Athenians to a naval policy. They protested when, at the height of the Persian invasion – as indeed often again during the Peloponnesian War which followed – they were urged to evacuate the rich lands of Attica and fight at sea. Their confidence, however, was restored by Cimon, the military leader, with a propaganda gesture. He offered up his horse's bridle to Athena, in the Acropolis, as a sign that Athens no longer needed horsemen and, taking a shield instead, walked down with it to the sea. It was a gesture symbolic of the city's future history.

Today Salamis is an island of fishermen. On the mainland, where Xerxes watched from his throne, the sea laps high against waterfront cafés and boat builders' yards, while the houses of the people, square and white and functional, spill in ever-increasing thousands up the tawny, barren hillside. Across the ferry, off the quarantine station where the fishermen prise oysters from the rocks, lie the relics of previous battles – disabled tank-landing craft from the Second World War; the hulk of a cruiser, with three strangely high funnels, from the First. On shore, open taxis of the Tin Lizzie vintage, their steering wheels elegantly plaited with raffia, ply for hire across dried-up hills to a wide and sheltered gulf, where the town of Salamis lies.

Here is the Greek joy in colour, which the sunlit landscape inspires. The houses of Salamis are washed a vivid ochre and blue, with shutters of clashing colours; their courtyards are bright with flowers and dark with fruit trees. In the village of Moulki the colour-washed cottages perch at random on whitewashed rocks, their vine-covered verandahs adorned with flowers in rows of whitewashed tins. By a café a Greek church stands among cypresses, its domes washed pink against rough blue-white walls.* On the road to a monastery a minute blue chapel crouches against the trunk of a giant protective cypress, a tree such as Xerxes himself would have revered, since, as a Persian, he coveted Europe in part for the repute of its garden trees.

Other trees – olive trees – dance down to the sea. Pine woods scent the northern headland, where the whitewashed monastery of Faneromeni, an array of irregular courts and arcades, looks back across the sea to the rich mainland, often in dispute in the past between Athens and the city of Megara. Today a tarmac road carries buses at breakneck speed through its flourishing fields and orchards, curving swiftly

* Plate, p. 41.

around the Gulf of Eleusis, where peasant families drive farm carts down to the sea to bathe in the cool of the evening.

Here lie the scattered ruins of the Eleusinian shrines, scene of those mysteries which stood for the more occult elements in the Greek religion – scene also, as such, of a bold venture by Alcibiades. Once, at the time of the annual celebration, when the surrounding territory was in the hands of the Spartans, he calmly scorned the alternative approach by sea, to lead a solemn procession along the Sacred Way through it, 'priests, novices, and initiates marching in the midst of his army, in great good order and perfect silence', to perform the accustomed rites. The enemy did not attack, and Alcibiades consolidated his rather shaky position, not only with the people but with the Goddess Athena, who had been thought to regard him with disfavour. Beyond Eleusis the road branches in two directions, towards Athens, whence he came, and towards Piraeus.

Before Salamis the Athenians kept their ships drawn up on the open beaches of Phaleron, where today they come in crowds from the city to swim in the sea and to bask in the sun and to drink in the shaded cafés. After the battle Themistocles, more than ever bent on his naval policy, completed the fortifications of this harbour of Piraeus as a permanent base for the fleet. It would perhaps have been best to abandon the Acropolis, seven miles inland, and to make Piraeus the capital, once and for all. But tradition and habit died hard: the conflict between landsmen and seamen, between Athena and Poseidon, persisted. Athens was reoccupied and had to be fortified too – in a hurry, moreover, with foundations made, according to Thucydides, 'of different sorts of stone, sometimes not shaped so as to fit, but laid down just as each was brought up at the time', with 'many pillars taken from tombs and fragments of sculpture mixed in with the rest'.

For the Athenians rightly feared aggression from their short-lived ally, Sparta. Aristophanes laughed at Themistocles for 'sticking Piraeus on to Athens'; but in fact Athens came to depend on Piraeus, which, as a centre of the new seafaring democracy, grew politically more and more powerful. Pericles laid out the city on the grid plan, lately devised by Hippodamus, an architect of Miletus, in Ionia, who tried, without success, to apply similar principles of symmetry to politics. It was the first city in Europe to be so designed, and created considerable interest among the Greeks. He built also the Long Walls, fortifications linking the port with Athens: walls which, at the final defeat of Athens, the Spartans, sparing the city itself, pulled down to the music of flute players, while, in the words of Plutarch, 'the allies crowned themselves with flowers and danced around, as though on that day their freedom began'. It was not, however, the end of Athens. The walls were to rise again – ironically under the auspices of a Persian satrap.

Today hardly a trace of them remains; nor a trace of the classical dignity of

ROMAN PROFUSION RATHER THAN GREEK RESTRAINT is shown by the sumptuous Corinthian columns of the Temple of Zeus Olympus. Deeply gilded by the sun, they throw off the severity of the Doric to flower abundantly with acanthus capitals.

Piraeus. Built on the grid plan still, but with ignoble, featureless streets, it is a jangling port, redeemed only by the two small harbours to the east of it, neat horseshoe basins alive with the masts and the rigging of sailing craft. But Piraeus has vigour, the rough animation of any southern port, transposed as it were into double rhythm by the restless vitality of the Greek. Sailors, brisk in their tight-cut uniforms, hurry through its streets; citizens and traders and loafers crowd its quays, alert with Greek curiosity as ship after ship comes swiftly in from the islands and worlds beyond. With the fall of darkness the whole wide crescent of Piraeus and Phaleron springs vividly to life; sky, sea and land become confused with a galaxy of stars and street lamps, the glow of the moon and the planets, the beam of a lighthouse, the phosphorescence of mauve neon lights.

Athens empties itself out to the sea, into taverns and cafés and cabarets which reek of it. Far into the neon-lit moonlit night, its citizens talk and eat octopus and drink their resinous wine; they dance, men and women together, to the amplified blare of an orchestra, men alone, in the abstracted sedate Greek style to the mandolin or the lute; they throng the open-air cinemas or the old puppet theatres, where traditional heroes and villains and clowns, silhouetted on a screen like grotesque caricatures of the figures on a classical vase, perform ludicrous antics, fight gory battles and orate in thunderous voices.

Where the Long Walls ran, a broad road carries them back to the city, buses racing one another like lumbering beasts, three abreast. Ahead of them the Acropolis arises, an ironclad of the land, confronting the sea; and on its bold hull of rock, so light as to seem to float in the sky, the floodlit columns of the Parthenon, memorial of victory, link in the chain between the Athens of history and the Europe of today.

'The Athenians', writes Thucydides, 'were the first to give up the habit of carrying weapons and to adopt a way of living that was more relaxed and more luxurious.' They laid the foundations of their power, after some centuries of Spartan supremacy, by a statesmanlike act: the union, under their rule, of the various small separate communities of Attica. In character they differed radically from the Spartans, as the Corinthians – again in the words of Thucydides – explained to them: 'An Athenian is always an innovator, quick to form a resolution and quick at carrying it out. You, on the other hand, are good at keeping things as they are; you never originate an idea, and your action tends to stop short of its aim. Then again Athenian daring will outrun its resources; they will take risks against their better judgment, and still, in the midst of danger, remain confident. But your nature is always to do less than you could have done, to mistrust your own judgment, however sound it may be, and to assume that dangers will last for ever. Think of this too: while you are hanging back, they never hesitate; while you stay at home, they

LOOKING DOWN FROM THE ACROPOLIS one sees a city unremarkable in design but bursting with vitality. At the very foot of the cliff sprawls the rambling quarter of the Plaka, part village, part slum.

are always abroad; for they think that the farther they go the more they will get, while you think that any movement may endanger what you have already.... Of them alone it may be said that they possess a thing almost as soon as they have begun to desire it, so quickly with them does action follow upon decision.'

Pericles, in his funeral oration after the outbreak of the war against Sparta, went further: 'We are lovers of the beautiful, yet simple in our tastes, and we cultivate the mind without loss of manliness ... to avow poverty with us is no disgrace; the true disgrace is in doing nothing to avoid it. ... We alone regard a man who takes no interest in public affairs, not as harmless, but as a useless character; and if few of us are originators, we are all sound judges of a policy. ... The individual Athenian in his own person seems to have the power of adapting himself to the most varied forms of action with the utmost versatility and grace.' Taste, enterprise, citizenship, versatility – such, in the words of their greatest ruler, were the characteristics of a people who evolved a society more civilized than any which has yet existed.

Athens lies in a plain, spreading up to the feet of three protective mountains: Pentelicon, Parnes and Hymettus. Smaller hills rise, in abrupt isolation, from the centre of it: the sharp cone of Licabettos, steep streets encroaching on its lower slopes; the wooded Pnyx, where the Athenians held their Parliament; the domed Areopagus, where their elders sat and where St Paul introduced to them his conception of the One God; the broad platform of the Acropolis itself, where they worshipped their own gods. Girt, in classical times, by two small streams, it was an ancient fortress and shrine, into which the Greeks introduced their own ancestral goddess Athena, threatening to oust Poseidon Erechtheus, the God of the Sea. After some dispute both deities were allowed, through a spirit of Greek compromise, to remain, she with her sacred olive tree, he with his salt spring, his sacred serpent, the marks of his trident in the rock. When Pericles, for fifteen years benevolent dictator of Athens, started to rebuild its temples as a thank-offering for the victory against the Persians, he built the Parthenon to the honour of Athena alone. But the older and more primitive Hecatompedon, with the relics of Erechtheus, survived ignobly at its side, still upheld by the more conservative priesthood, until, some years after his death, it was finally replaced by the Erechtheion.

Pericles employed Phidias as overseer and manager of his building programme, which was largely completed in his lifetime. It was carried out, not by mass slave labour, like the building of the Pyramids, but, with typical Greek individualism, by thousands of small contractors, each employing a few craftsmen and masons and slaves of his own. The sculpture, as on the pediments and frieze of the temple, was the work of a team of men, working under general direction, receiving a flat rate of sixty drachmas per figure. The Parthenon was thus a work inherently democratic in execution, the work of the people as a whole. Pericles was severely criticized for extravagance, 'for gilding and beautifying one city as if it were a vain woman', more especially as he used funds which had been contributed by the Allies for the purpose of the war. He argued however that Athens, having defended them effectively, had the right to spend any surplus as it wished. Why not 'by the erection of buildings which would be a glory to it for all ages' and would at the same time relieve unemployment?

'The different materials used,' says Plutarch, 'such as stone, brass, ivory, gold, ebony, cypress wood, and so forth, would require special artisans for each, such as carpenters, modellers, smiths, stone masons, dyers, melters and moulders of gold, and ivory painters, embroiderers, workers in relief; and also men to bring them to the city, such as sailors and captains of ships and pilots for such as came by sea; and for those who came by land, carriage builders, horse breeders, drivers, rope makers, linen manufacturers, shoemakers, road menders and miners. Each trade, moreover, employed a number of unskilled labourers, so that, in a word, there would be work for persons of every age and every class, and general prosperity would be the result.' The enemies of Pericles further alleged that he and Phidias carried on intrigues with the Athenian ladies who came to see the works, and a bird-fancying friend of his was said to reward them, on his behalf, with peacocks. Scorning these imputations he finally offered, with a lordly gesture, to pay for all the buildings out of his own pocket, and inscribe his name on them. Thus the opposition was silenced and the work proceeded. Phidias himself carved a huge wooden-helmeted statue of Athena, in ivory and gold, for the interior of the Parthenon, which, like the rest of his work, has vanished; he may also have helped to design the sculptured pediment and frieze for its exterior. The temple itself was designed by Ictinos; the Propylae by Mnesicles.

The Propylae, the gates of the Acropolis, stand at the head of a steep broad stairway, climbing the western cliff, whose naked rock still projects beside the well-trodden steps. It is an ascent, suitably slow and laborious, to a pillared hall still screening the temple from view. On a spur to the right there stands, at an angle, a miniature temple, like a chapel on the threshold of a cathedral, a reflection of the grander shrine to come. It is the temple of Athena Nike, the Wingless Victory, symbolizing not merely the defeat of the Persians but an earlier victory still. From this outcrop of rock, looking down over the plain and the broad expanse of the Saronic Gulf beyond, Aegeus, King of ancient Athens, watched for the return of his son Theseus, who had sailed for Crete to kill the Minotaur, and so liberate Athens from her dependence on the imperialist King Minos. Theseus had promised to hoist a white sail in the event of victory, and a black one in the event of defeat, but forgot his promise, in his distress at losing Ariadne, and sailed up the Gulf with a black sail at his mast. Aegeus thereupon flung himself down from the rock, to his death. After their final liberation from the threat of the invader, at Salamis, the Greeks were determined that Victory should never elude them again, so symbolically clipped its wings, in their dedication of this shrine.

The columns of the Propylae lead through into an open world of space and light and silence. Here the rock, plastered smooth by time, bleached white by the sun, slopes gently up to the broad stone floor where the Parthenon, in serene isolation, raises its columns and pediments to the sky. Quarried from the marble of Pentelicon, coloured and moulded by the sun and the winds for the past two thousand years and more, the temple stands on its rock as though compounded of the natural elements of light and earth and air, distilled into stone, but still instinct with their life and movement. It is a stone moreover alive with their changing spectrum of colour – its fluted surfaces now grey as the clouds, now gold as the sunlight, now white as the moonlight. But even in ruins – perhaps more than ever in ruins – the Parthenon remains in its essence a distillation of the human spirit, a consummate compound of the conflicting elements in the mind and heart of man. Here reason and emotion, the human and the divine, are for once resolved and crystallized into an enduring work of art.*

The Parthenon is a synthesis of opposites. Planted firmly on the ground, it yet seems to soar into space. Profoundly simple in effect, it is infinitely complex in conception, its flawless proportions the product of intricate mathematical thought. It is never what it seems. What at first sight looks rigid is revealed as elastic; where a column or an entablature look straight they are curved; where two columns look identical in size, they are different. The building is like a work by Bach or Handel, transposed into plastic form. Through the discipline of a stern intellectual process, it conveys a supreme sense of emotional liberation.

Humanity is inherent in its architecture. Vitruvius relates Greek architectural proportions to those of the human body. In these terms the Theseum – standing on the fringe of the Agora at the foot of the Acropolis rock – is, with its sterner lines, essentially masculine. The Parthenon, on the other hand, is at once masculine and feminine. To achieve perfection of form, the Athenians have here adopted the order of the Dorians, with all its manly vigour, and have infused it with the more feminine grace of the order of the Ionians – those Achaeans who fled from the Dorian invasions of Greece to the gentler lands of Asia Minor. In this symbol of their victory of West against East, they thus reconcile, in terms of art, as indeed they were to do in terms of history, the qualities of either world. As though to point the contrast, there stands, apart from the Parthenon, the Erechtheion, a temple essentially feminine, with its slender Ionic columns, and its portico embodying six virgin female figures.

Little other Greek sculpture remains on the Acropolis: its relics are dispersed among the museums of the world, but especially in the National Museum of

* Frontispiece, and p. 42.

Athens itself. Here, in statues and reliefs, it can be traced throughout the various phases of its rise and decline, together with the arts of celature and painting on vases, at which the Greeks, inspired initially by the Minoans, excelled. Here, in successive centuries, are the statues of gods as gods, of gods as men, of men as gods, of men as men. First come the Archaic figures of the seventh century B.C., with their stylized bodies and other-world smiles, still formal in the manner of the Egyptians, from whom the wandering Greeks derived inspiration; next the figures, freer and more truly Greek, of the fifth century, the zenith of classical art, when gods were depicted in a living human form; next those of the fourth century, essentially now of human beings, but still with a flame of divinity; finally the figures of the Hellenistic period, now purely realistic, ideas degenerating into sentiment, sensuality and illusions of reality, until classical sculpture reaches the nadir of Roman commercial mass production.

Here are works of art retrieved by archaeologists from the earth and by fishermen from the sea. Here are Poseidon or Zeus, from the waters of Cape Artemisium, an Ephebe from Antikythera, Hermes from Marathon, a boy jockey again from Artemisium, their bronze limbs glowing green and gold and black from the action, throughout the centuries, of the elements far down on the sea bed. As within the walls of the Acropolis Greek divinity and humanity are here enshrined for posterity.

From the Romans to Lord Elgin

The Romans, in capturing Athens, spared the Parthenon, in view of the city's former glories. But they carried off its treasure, together with some columns of the Temple of Zeus Olympus, beneath the rock, a building which had been started on a grandiose scale by Peisistratus, a predecessor of Pericles, but never finished. It was finished later by Hadrian, an emperor who, like Herodes Atticus, admired Greek art, restored a number of ancient buildings, and enriched the remainder of the city with public works in the Roman manner. Its sumptuous Corinthian columns, deeply gilded by the sun, throwing off the severity of the Doric to flower abundantly with acanthus capitals, still survive as a frame for the purer outlines of the Parthenon, floating lightly above it, as though to point an ironic contrast between Roman profusion and Greek restraint.* It is pointed further by the fleshly statues of Roman gods and goddesses around the theatre of Dionysus, once the austere centre of Greek religious drama, carved out of the base of the Acropolis rock. Herodes Atticus earned the ridicule of the Athenians by ostentatiously covering the seats of the stadium with marble, from the profits of his tax extortions.

The city of Athens continued, throughout Roman times, to be respected as a centre of learning. When it was captured by the Goths they refrained from burning

* Plate, p. 47.

its libraries, on the argument of a soldier who suggested that the Athenians would be more harmless employed over their books than over warlike exercises. In Byzantine times its schools of philosophy, slowly lapsing into pedantry, were finally closed in the sixth century by Justinian, and the last of the Athenian philosophers, heirs of the ancient classical tradition, were exiled to Persia. Already a traveller had remarked that, instead of philosophers in the Agora, you met only dealers in honey. Athens dwindled into obscurity, so that sixteenth-century travellers described it, doubtless inaccurately, as a mere village, haunted by wolves and other wild beasts, while Piraeus was no more than a huddle of fishermen's huts.

But the Parthenon survived. It was converted into a Christian church, dedicated to the Virgin Mary, with Byzantine paintings on its walls. So the Crusaders found it, untouched by time and hardly injured by man. They desecrated it, and adapted it to the Catholic rite, while the Dukes of Athens built themselves a palace over the columns of the Propylae. The Turks turned it into a mosque, complete with minaret. At the end of the seventeenth century it was still intact. But when Morosini and his Venetians besieged the Acropolis, the Temple of the Wingless Victory was removed to make room for a Turkish battery. One of their bombs then fell on the Propylae, blowing up a powder magazine; another fell on the Parthenon itself, where the Turks had deposited their valuables, together with powder and inflammable stores.

'A terrific explosion took place; the centre columns of the peristyle, the walls of the cella, and the immense architraves and cornices they supported, were scattered around the remains of the temple. Much of the unrivalled sculpture was defaced and a part utterly destroyed. The materials heaped up in the building also took fire, and the flames, mounting high over the Acropolis, announced the calamity to the besiegers, and scattered many of the statues which still remained in their original positions.' So wrote the historian, Finlay. So Athens fell to Venice, and the Parthenon was no more. Early in the nineteenth century Lord Elgin, Ambassador in Constantinople, with the permission of the Turks and to the scorn of Lord Byron, removed the greater part of the frieze, which might otherwise have been removed by another, and sold it at a loss to the British Museum. But the Parthenon can hardly be said to have perished. Its perfection of form survives its ruins, giving it a quality of permanence unsurpassed by any other work of the hand of man.

Christian shrines

The Acropolis, with its stout medieval walls, rises up like a dreadnought above the roofs and the courtyards and the streets of modern Athens. Built to replace a small market town, by the architects of King Otho in the nineteenth century, it is an undistinguished city, designed on a monotonous grid-plan, without due relation to Licabettos or the Acropolis, the hills which are its natural feature. Here are neither the boulevards of Paris nor the fountains and cool arcades of Rome. Its interminable canyons of streets lack character; its squares are adorned by neo-classical buildings of poor inspiration and unhappy proportions. It is moreover an overpopulated city. The Greeks are a gregarious race, essentially urban in character, who pour into their capital in mounting numbers, preferring poverty to the tedium of the islands and the countryside, then spill out of it again towards the sea and the mountains, in an agglomeration of makeshift suburbs. The pavements of Athens are for ever dense with hustling crowds; its traffic drives without thought of pedestrians, as though to kill. It is a city redeemed only by its royal and public gardens, shady with thickets of aromatic trees; by the occasional unforeseen glimpse of a rustic backyard, amid the glare of the concrete and steel, planted with trees to make an outdoor tavern; by the wide open spaces of Constitution Square, the Agora of today, its offices blinking with neon advertisements for air lines, radios, tooth-pastes, its café tables, where thousands talk, shaded and scented by pollarded orange trees.

But it is a city which bursts with vitality. At night it spreads out from the foot of the Acropolis, the life of it surging, the sound of it lapping around the silent moonlit rock. Right up to the foot of it sprawls the Plaka, an unending, moving jigsaw of light and darkness, the rambling quarter, part village, part slum, which survives from Turkish times.* Bright in the daylight, beneath its red tiled roofs, with clotheslines, pot-flowers, pedlars' wares, its courtyards and streets are now wedges and fissures of light, from which distinctive sounds – the cry of a child, the bray of a donkey, the bark of a dog – drift upwards. Lighted rooms stand empty as families, unashamed in pyjamas, move beds and chairs outside, to get a grandstand view of a neighbouring rooftop tavern, its tables pinpoints of light amid a hubbub of talk, the twang of a mandolin, the song of an itinerant musician. Over all, symbol of a life more eternal, the temple presides in muted dignity, its fluted columns white in the moonlight, merging into a soft night sky.

Athens has other, Christian shrines. In the heart of the city small Byzantine churches and chapels crouch at the foot of towering concrete buildings. On the road out of it, where suddenly the city ends in the broad scented slopes of Hymettus (now replanted with young trees after the destruction of its forests by the Germans), is the monastery of Kaisariani.† Built in a secluded gorge, by the sweet waters of a fountain praised by Ovid, it stands in a garden of roses and honeysuckle, beneath the ample shade of plane and pine, its rough tiled roofs bizarre in their patterns of sun-baked ridge and furrow.

On the road to Eleusis is the convent church of Daphni, built in the eleventh century among the groves which once shaded a classical temple of Apollo.† Its weathered

* Plate, p. 48.   † Plate, p. 57.

stone walls stand amid orchards in a cloistered courtyard, beneath a pine-clad slope. Long narrow windows add height to the church, their lattices honeycombs of gypsum, relieving its severity with light brick architraves in a variety of geometrical patterns. Before its tall façade rises a pair of guardian cypresses, taller still, their trunks slender as columns, their tapering branches flanking the dome like steeples.

Within, the shadowy darkness of the high, narrow vaults comes to life with the glow of mosaics in luminous blues and golds: while the classical Greeks adorned mainly the exterior of their temples, for all to see, the Christian Greeks preferred, behind an unadorned exterior, to beautify the house of their God within, thus intensifying, in the mind of the worshipper, the awe created by the beauty of the service, and enriching its ritual with an intimate visual picture of the heavenly hierarchy and the events of the Christian story. Gracing the domes and the niches, the pendentives and the curved wall spaces of Daphni – architecture as it were designed for them alone – gods become men, as the classical Golden Age portrayed them, but with a hieratic formalism familiar in a more archaic age. The Christ and Virgin, Saints and Prophets combine in their style the grace of the pagan Greek with the mystery of the Semitic gods of the East. The deep sunk eyes and the bearded features of the Christ Pantocrator, who fills the dome, are those of an all-seeing oriental divinity. But his sacred followers, white-bearded figures in black and white robes, beneath canopies of gleaming gold, have a Greek humanity, as of philosophers, scientists, men of letters. Even their names have a classical ring: St Bacchus, for instance, with his sword and sceptre; other saints, now forgotten, whose Greek names may be translated in such human terms as St Non-Dangerous, St Hope-Bringing. The scenes moreover from the Bible story – the wise men, with the ox and the ass, at the manger, the boyish Christ in the temple, the adult Christ bathing in the waters of the Jordan – have, for all their mystic solemnity, the aspect of every-day scenes in the visible sunlit world without.

An Acropolis of the Sea

Between Hymettus and Pentelicon the rich lands of Attica, so often and so reluctantly abandoned by the Athenians to the enemy, run away south-east towards the open Aegean and the islands strung out across it. Here is a valley abundant with olives and wines and fields of corn, the crops overflowing up the red hillsides and slashing them vividly green. The sea beckons from the end of it, a streamer of blue, and here, facing the island of Makronisi, where political prisoners languish, is the mining district of Lavrion. It was from the silver of these mines – once the source of the Athenian coinage of 'Lavriot Owls', now the source mainly of zinc and manganese – that Themistocles was able to finance the building of the Athenian fleet,

CHRISTIAN AS WELL AS PAGAN SHRINES are part of the Athenian country side, varying from the rough, sun-baked tiles of the Kaisariani monastery t the church of Daphni, elegant, cypress-guarded, withdrawn.

FISHERMAN OF AEGINA. His stubborn, courageous island ancestors blocked the seaward expansion of Athens 2,300 years ago, but later they helped to defeat the Persian
armada at Salamis. The sea was in their blood, as it is in his.

before Salamis. The slave-workers in the mines later rebelled, with some success, against the tyranny of the Romans, an outbreak of social discontent matched by others in Sicily and different parts of Greece.

South of Lavrion the mainland of Greece breaks off in a defiant, vertical headland. This is Cape Sunion, where Poseidon at length comes into his own. His temple, crowning a natural Acropolis of the sea, commands the waves and the winds of the Aegean as that of Athena commands the Athenian plain. Stepped up, since the days of Pericles, on a platform of rough gold stone, its bright white columns, carved from a local Attic marble, are so encrusted and worn as to seem compounded of the sea foam, crystallized and glazed with the salt spray of twenty-four centuries. On one of their stones is carved a signature reputed to be that of Lord Byron. To him Sunion was Cape Colonna, the scene not merely of some of Plato's conversations, but of the shipwreck of a lesser English poet, Falconer, who wrote:

> But now the Athenian Mountains they descry,
> And o'er the surge Colonna frowns on high;
> Beside the cape's projecting verge is plac'd
> A range of columns, long by time defac'd;
> First planted by devotion to sustain,
> In elder times, Tritonia's sacred fame.

Spread at their feet is a glittering prospect of headlands and islands: the whole wide arc of the Saronic Gulf, and, to the east of it, the Cyclades, stepping across to the coast of Asia Minor. Here, in short, beneath the guardian pillars of Sunion, is that empire of the seas which was at once the glory and the ruin of classical Athens.

5

Islands of the Aegean

The first main obstacle to the maritime expansion of Athens – and indeed in a sense its occasion – was the island of Aegina, placed in strategic position in the heart of the Saronic Gulf. The graceful cone of its mountain, matching the lines of Pentelicon, was to Athenians 'the eyesore of the Piraeus'. A Dorian settlement, Aegina was a commercial power before Athens, which indeed adopted the Aeginetan coinage. In view of her unprovoked aggressions on the coasts of Attica, and moreover of her apparent leanings towards Persia, Athens first called upon Sparta to put pressure on the Aeginetans and later, without conclusive result, sent a fleet to attack them. Aegina redeemed herself at Salamis, fighting well for the Greeks. She did well out of the Battle of Plataea, buying golden booty from the ignorant serfs at the price of brass. Later, in two major naval engagements, Athens defeated Aegina, and, on the outbreak of the Peloponnesian War, disposed of her once and for all, expelling the whole population and annexing the island to Attica. At a later stage in Greek history Demosthenes, banished from Athens, after the manner of Greek statesmen, for corruption, spent part of his exile on the island, looking across towards Attica with tears in his eyes. On leaving Athens he had apostrophized Athena: 'Why dost thou delight in those three savage creatures, the owl, the snake and the people?'

Today a swift service of boats plies backwards and forwards between Aegina, no longer an eyesore, and Piraeus. The slopes of the island are scattered with chapels and crowned with the temple of Aphaea, built to honour a local goddess and commemorate the part played by Aegina at the Battle of Salamis.* Its refined Doric columns, rising to a second tier as in the triforium of a church, soar high above pine trees, commanding the sunlit expanse of the Gulf as the ships of Aegina could once claim to do. Beneath it, amid the scent of pines and sea, the Aeginetans now come to bathe, around the tranquil sweep of a bay.

Originally Aegina was subject to Epidaurus, on the Argolid coast of the Saronic

* Plate, p. 63.

Gulf. But the Aeginetans, growing stronger at sea, rebelled against their masters and removed two of their most sacred statues. Made from Athenian olive wood, the statues carried an obligation to pay tribute to Athens, which the Aeginetans now refused to fulfil. The Athenians, according to their own story, thus sent a warship to seize the statues, on the grounds that, being of Athenian wood, they were Athenian property. 'First', writes Herodotus, 'they tried to wrench them off their pedestals; then, having failed to do so, they made ropes fast to them, and hauled. As they were heaving there was a clap of thunder and an earthquake, and the ship's company suddenly went mad and began to kill each other, until only one was left, who returned by himself to Phalerum.' The Aeginetan story is that the Athenians sent not a ship but a fleet, which was allowed to land unopposed. When the sailors were trying to heave the statues away, 'each statue fell upon its knees, and in that attitude both have remained ever since.' Argive reinforcements, from Epidaurus, then fell upon the Athenians.

When the sole Athenian survivor of the operation reached Athens, 'the wives of the other men who had gone with him to Aegina ... crowded round him and thrust the brooches, which they used for fastening their dresses, into his flesh, each one, as she struck, asking him where her husband was. So the poor fellow was killed, and the Athenians were more horrified at his fate than at the defeat of their troops in Aegina. The only way they could punish their women for the dreadful thing they had done was to make them adopt Ionian dress; previously Athenian women had worn Dorian dress, very similar to the fashion at Corinth; now they were made to change to linen tunics, to prevent them from wearing brooches.' The Argives and Aeginetans, on the other hand, decreed that in future brooch-pins should be made half as long again as they used to be.

Epidaurus lies inland from a sheltered bay, where boys bathe off the rocks, and a tavern serves fish straight from the sea. Here, over a wide expanse, lie the ruined baths and temples of a spa, where Greeks and Romans came to be cured of their ailments by Asclepios, the 'blameless physician' of Homer, who was afterwards revered as a god. Born here in secret, a child of Apollo, he was exposed by his mother, the daughter of a Boeotian King, on the slopes of a mountain, but was suckled and kept alive by a herd of goats. Hence the reputation of Epidaurus as a health resort. Furnished with a hospital, with houses for the doctors, and buildings where the patients could engage in gymnastic and musical exercises, it became the prototype of other such salubrious settlements as far afield as Pergamum and Smyrna. Wherever they went the Epidaurian colonists carried with them the divine physician's sacred serpent: on one occasion, during a destructive plague, they carried it as far as Rome.

The mountain on which the infant god lay exposed provides a backcloth, shadowed with pines and ribbed with limestone, for a theatre, one of the largest in the classical world. Rising steeply up a hillside, radiating tier above tier in a wide stepped crescent of stone, it was built to seat fourteen thousand people – and indeed still on occasion does so. For the Greeks have restored it, and revive here each summer the plays of the classical masters. From Athens and the islands and all parts of the Peloponnese they flock here, by boat and by bus, as though for some major sporting event. Amid the smell of trodden grass, to the sound of Greek loudspeakers, they file in their thousands, past the car-parks, the first-aid tents, the stalls of bottled minerals, up to the theatre which saw its first first-night some two thousand three hundred years ago.

Crowding the hot stone seats, young Greeks in shirt-sleeves, girls in flowery skirts, peasant families in fustian, with old crones in black – to say nothing of an American in jeans, a German in lederhosen, an Englishman dressed as though for the opera – they sit waiting, amid a hubbub of expectation, while the sun goes slowly down behind them, gilding the pine trees and deepening the mountain shadows. Presently, as the dusk falls, the goddess Aphrodite, floodlit gold, materializes on a pedestal, reciting the prologue, creating an instant, reverent hush. Then, as the sun sets and the moon slowly rises, the audience leans forward in a mood of enthralled concentration, absorbing a tragic drama of incest, violent death and remorse. It is the work of a familiar and favourite playwright, Euripides.

The eyes of Poros

Beyond Epidaurus, its hillsides terraced like an amphitheatre, but now for the cultivation of olives and vines, lies the more modern health resort of Methana, known for its sulphurous baths. A row of houses on the sea, with an hotel or two and the cupola of a blue church rising behind, it stands on a volcanic peninsula which is almost an island, and indeed virtually became one when the Athenians built a wall across its isthmus, during the Peloponnesian War. Beyond Methana the coast line softens into orchards and meadows, luminous and green beneath a blue range of mountains, its profile suggesting the contours of some vast recumbent goddess. Before it groups of poplars arise, silvery green reflections of the darker cypresses, standing upright as sentries above the roofs of whitewashed farmsteads. Blue shadows pour down over rounded hillsides, lightly cushioned with pines. Framed in this fertile Italianate setting is an almost land-locked gulf, pellucid and still as a lagoon.

The ship turns suddenly into it, around a headland of rock, and there ahead of her, a stylized ballet-set dramatically revealed by the rise of a curtain, the island of Poros thrusts forward, its town stepped up over a bare hillside like some arrogant

ON THE ISLANDS OF THE AEGEAN. A headless Athenian Cleopatra and her husband, on Delos; the archaic, stylized Delian lion; the graceful double columns of Aegina's Temple of Aphaea; the harmonious cubes and spheres of a modern church on Mykonos.

THE PORT OF HYDRA lies, compact and shipshape, within the embrace of two strong arms of rock, rising steep from the sea, encircled with tier above tier of tall grey houses.

cubist ant-heap. All eyes, it stares the stranger in the face with an alive curiosity, families crowding to its balconies as the ship sails beneath them, passengers peering into rooms lit by the sea, at a life lived openly, Greek and unashamed. It is an island typical of the Greek seafaring spirit, the people of Poros defiantly preferring their barren rocks to the luxuriant mainland plain, with its orchards of lemons.

Visitors from Athens crowd to Poros. In the evenings, as the light which flooded it fades, nature yields wholly to the theatre, with flamboyant red skies, deep violet mountains, and a lagoon which becomes a silken mantle of silver, shot with amethyst lights and adorned with a pattern of turquoise boats. As, in the Romantic manner, the moon rides up over the island's pine-clad hillside, a thyme-scented stillness descends on the water, broken far into the night as the sound of Greek music drifts over it from the boats and lamplit waterfront taverns.

The shipbuilders of Hydra

No two islands in the Aegean are alike. Miniature city states still, isolated by water, each differs from the other in aspect and character as distinctly as Athens once differed from Sparta or Corinth from Thebes. Many indeed, under the Turks, retained a fair degree of independence. The inhabitants of Poros are sociable, easy-going, refined and it may be a trifle corrupted by the supple Athenian ways. The inhabitants of Hydra, its southern neighbour, are dour, independent, silent by Greek standards, straightforward and stern in their dealings. They are in fact of Albanian origin, a race which fled from Epirus to the Peloponnese during the Turkish invasions of the fifteenth century, and was well established on the island by the eighteenth. It is a barren island, ill-supplied with water. Hence the Turks exempted the Hydriots from taxation, and enabled them in effect to manage their own internal affairs like a small independent republic. It was a republic strongly oligarchical in character, dominated by a few rich shipowning families. For the Hydriots had turned from their barren lands to the sea, and in time built up a substantial merchant navy. They first grew rich running the British blockade to carry supplies to Napoleon during the Nile campaign.

A democratic tradition prevailed in the ships themselves, whose crews had a share in the cargo, with a percentage for the municipality and the church. Thus, in the event of a dangerous enterprise, they would hold a council on board to decide whether the Captain's orders should be obeyed. When the Greek revolt started, the Hydriots were able to supply the rebels with a ready-made fleet, which played a vital part in the War of Independence. On occasion, piratical by nature, they treated their Turkish prizes with a brutality worthy of classical times, recalling the days when the Athenians exterminated the inhabitants of Melos and the Spartans slaughtered their Athenian prisoners after winning the Peloponnesian War at the Battle of Aegospotami.

But the Hydriots created an island civilization all their own, surviving today in the perfection of its architectural style. The port of Hydra lies, compact and ship-shape, within the embrace of two strong arms of rock. Bleached grey, weathered gold, spread with dry gold earth, it is a rock, rising steep from the sea, which the Hydriots have quarried to encircle their harbour with tier above tier of tall grey houses.* Craftsmen have pointed the stone with golden mortar, roofed it with sun-baked earthen tiles, relieved its austerity, here with whitewash, there with windows and shutters of pastel blues and buffs and greys, but never with colours more ostentatious. Each individual has built as he chose, but within the collective limits of an ordered tradition, dignified proportions and a restrained, well-mannered style. Grey and white walls, zigzagging over the hillside, divide one man's property from another's. Quays are evenly paved, their flags picked out here and there with white-wash to make a checkerboard pattern. Doorsteps and stairways are freshly white-washed or pink-washed, and for ever cleanly scrubbed by house-proud women, as the men scrub the decks of their ships. The trunk of a fig tree, the corner of a wall, have been used as a palette, all streaked with reds and greens and blues by the painters of fishing boats, brightly reflected in the lapping translucent water. Panelled doors, well-moulded and adorned with knockers, lead into the precincts of the statelier homes of the Hydriot thalassocracy. From gardens and courtyards vaulted halls lead on into rooms with fretted wood ceilings, thence into loggias command-ing the sea and the harbour which brought their families first mercantile wealth, then naval distinction, in the newborn state of Greece.

Tradition decrees that no wheeled vehicle, not even a wheelbarrow, bicycle or perambulator, shall desecrate the island of Hydra. Thus none but pedestrians grace its waterfront, busy by day with shops and stalls selling tomatoes and egg-plants, sponges and fishermen's gear, alive by night with the tables of taverns and cafés, right to the water's edge. Here no radio blares, but only the occasional music of a mandolin and a continuous echoing hubbub of talk. Sounds of traffic are the sounds of boats alone, their motors chugging in and out of the harbour with a monotonous rhythm. Neither roads nor cart tracks wind up over the hillside: only broad cobbled paths, marching directly upwards, where mules and donkeys alone carry their masters' loads. Beyond the town abandoned windmills, like Venetian watch towers, line a treeless ridge, still white with houses, and falling into a sequence of miniature bays. Here the shingle resolves into a neat mosaic pavement beneath a transparent carpet of water, while in the green and blue depths, amid fronds of sea-weed, fishes revolve in shoals, veering this way and that like clouds of leaves in the sky. At sundown the sea becomes an iridescent floor, the islands upon it turning

* Plate, p. 64.

slowly to black, the white chapels which crown them to purple, while the surrounding panorama, its perspective no longer confined by the sun, unfolds in depth, disclosing in a progression of darkening blues layer behind layer of Peloponnesian mountains.

Decline of the Athenian Empire

The initial instrument of the Athenian Empire of the seas was the Confederacy of Delos. This was a naval league, formed for defensive purposes, with its headquarters and treasury on the sacred island of Delos, strategically placed in the centre of the Aegean. It was at first a voluntary association of independent states, for the most part islands, each contributing to Athens, as the executive authority, either ships or a cash payment for its defence. Inevitably Athens, with far the largest number of ships, came to dominate the league, forcing new states into it and treating harshly those which wished to secede. Finally the headquarters was transferred from Delos to Athens, and the transformation into an Empire was complete.

At first it was an Empire which served, well enough, the interests of its member-states. But as time went on they felt their freedom unduly restricted, and began openly to grumble of Athenian tyranny. This enabled Sparta to emerge, with some initial effect, as the champion of Greek liberties. In the course of the war between them the Athenians had revolts on their hands. The rebels of Mitylene appealed to Sparta (in the words of Thucydides): 'The object of the alliance was the liberation of the Hellenes from Persia, not the subjugation of the Hellenes to Athens'; in wartime the Athenians 'did their best to be on good terms with us because they were frightened of us; we, for the same reason, tried to keep on good terms with them in peacetime. In most cases good will is the basis of loyalty, but in our case fear was the bond, and it was more through terror than through friendship that we were held together in alliance.'

In threatening force, to coerce the people of Melos into alliance with them, the Athenians frankly abandoned 'fine phrases, saying, for example, that we have a right to our empire because we defeated the Persians', and resorted to arguments of realist expediency: 'You know as well as we do that when these matters are discussed by practical people, the standard of justice depends on the quality of power to compel and that in fact the strong do what they have the power to do and the weak accept what they have to accept.' The following dialogue ensued:

ATHENIANS ... We do not want any trouble in bringing you into our empire, and we want you to be spared for the good both of yourselves and of ourselves.

MELIANS: And how could it be just as good for us to be the slaves as for you to be the masters?

ATHENIANS: You, by giving in, would save yourselves from disaster; we, by not destroying you, would be able to profit from you.

MELIANS: So you would not agree to our being neutral, friends instead of enemies, but allies of neither side?

ATHENIANS: No, because it is not so much your hostility that injures us; it is rather the case that, if we were on friendly terms with you, our subjects would regard that as a sign of weakness in us, whereas your hatred is evidence of our power.

Power slowly corrupted Athens; an excess of imperialist ambition finally ruined her. Alcibiades, in initiating the disastrous Sicilian expedition, fanned its flames. According to Plutarch, 'he raised great expectations among the people, but his own aspirations were far more extensive; for he regarded the conquest of Sicily not merely as an end, but as a stepping stone to greater things ... Alcibiades was dreaming of Carthage and Libya, and after these were gained he meditated the conquest of Italy and of Peloponnesus, regarding Sicily as little more than a convenient magazine and place of arms. He greatly excited the younger Athenians by his vast designs, and they listened eagerly to the marvellous stories of the old who had served in that country; so that many of them would spend their time sitting in the gymnasia and public seats drawing sketches of the island of Sicily and of the position of Libya and Carthage.'

But Socrates foresaw disaster, and his instinct was right. Thucydides describes the final tragedy, when 'the whole army was filled with tears and in such distress of mind that they found it difficult to go away from this land of their enemies where sufferings too great for tears had befallen them and more still, they feared, awaited them in the dark future ahead ... No Hellenic army had ever suffered such a reverse. They had come to enslave others, and now they were going away frightened of being enslaved themselves.' The failure of the expedition hastened the decline and fall of the Athenian Empire, after a mere fifty years of life.

The Spartan Empire, which followed it, endured for an even shorter period, since the Spartans were a high-handed race, with no notion of the government of democratic peoples. The attempt of the Greek city-states to combine, except when faced by a common danger, had failed, in a sense because of their inherent merit: that spirit of independence which shrank from a voluntary and resented a compulsory surrender of sovereignty. After the partial recovery of Athens – as a city if no longer as an empire – followed by a brief period of Theban predominance, their free and highly civilized system was to give way before the more cosmopolitan nationalist conception, first of Alexander, a monarch of the old Patriarchal school, and finally of alien and imperial Rome.

STOUT, THATCHED WINDMILLS guard the hilltops around Mykonos, their wide
wheels creaking, their little triangular sails flapping in the wind.

THE HARBOUR OF MYKONOS. Taverns and tourist shops, a chapel and the Apollo Hotel,
all shining with sunlit whitewash, frame a picture patterned with gaily painted boats.

Delos: the island of Apollo

The island of Delos rose dramatically from the sea at the touch of Poseidon and, after drifting for a period, was chained down by Zeus, to become a refuge for Latona and thus the birthplace of Apollo and Artemis. According to Pliny it has been called also Cynthus, Quail Island, Star Island, Hare Island, Cloak Island, Dog Island, and Fiery Island, 'because fire was first discovered there'. The ruins of its cities lie scattered over a broad and grassy sward, then stepped up over the rocky grey slopes of a pointed hill. Since the island became Apollo's holiest shrine, and never lost its sacred character, they cover a wide span of history, from the heroic age of Homer to the commercial age of Rome.

A wandering progress from one epoch to another, from the Agora of the Romans to the temple precincts of the fifth-century Athenians, through the streets of the Alexandrine period up to the cave hewn out of the mountainside in the Mycenaean style, reveals innumerable foundations and plinths and columns, Ionic and Doric, together with fragments of carving and statuary: here an immense Roman torso, there a phallus on a pedestal, here a headless Athenian Cleopatra with headless husband.* By the Sacred Lake, a notable amenity of Apollo's temple which was filled in only a generation ago, stands the terrace of the lions, a row of archaic stone beasts, long and lean as greyhounds, stylized as the works of some modern sculptor.* On the slopes of the hill, gathered around the theatre, stand a number of elegant houses – the House of the Dolphins, of the Masks, of Cleopatra, of the Trident – containing mosaics in a sophisticated style. From its summit a temple of Zeus and Athena, graced with a mosaic dedication, surveys a majestic panorama of deep green sea, the shadowy forms of islands hovering above the horizon as though in the sky.

The nearest, across a narrow strait, is Rhenea. So near is it that Polycrates, the Samian tyrant, dedicated it to Apollo by binding it to Delos with a chain. It was here that Datis, the Persian general, landed, respecting the sanctity of Delos itself. The Delians, who had evacuated the island at his approach, received a message from him, recorded by Herodotus: 'Sirs, what strange opinion have you conceived of me, thus to abandon your sacred home? I surely have sense enough – even without the King's orders – to spare the island in which Apollo and Artemis were born, and to do no harm either to its soil or its people.' He then burnt some £75,000 worth of frankincense as an offering to Apollo. Later, on his return voyage to Asia, he discovered in one of his ships a statue of Apollo, overlaid with gold, which had been looted from a temple in Theban territory. He landed it at Delos, for safe keeping, instructing the inhabitants to return it to its rightful owners. They preferred however to keep it, until it was finally recovered by the Thebans themselves.

* Plate, p. 63.

When the Athenians, in response to an oracle during the Peloponnesian War, purified Delos, they dug up all the dead from its tombs, and decreed that in future all those who were about to die or give birth should do so on Rhenea itself. They then introduced a festival of Delian games, as the Ionians had done before them, inspiring the Homeric Hymn to Apollo:

> *Chiefly, O Phoebus, your heart found delight in the island of Delos.*
> *There, with their long robes trailing, Ionians gather together*
> *Treading your sacred road, with their wives and their children about them,*
> *There they give you pleasure with boxing and dancing and singing,*
> *Calling aloud on your name, as they set in order the contests.*

Later in the war, considering this purification inadequate, they evacuated all the inhabitants from Delos, on the grounds that they were still in a state of pollution, from an ancient offence. But, as the war went badly, they moved them back, in response to advice from Delphi.

In the seventeenth century Delos was looted, for the benefit of Charles I, by Sir Kenelm Digby, a gentleman privateer, who brought him back 'old Greek marble vases, columns and altars' from the temple of Apollo. He was following the example of the British Ambassador in Constantinople, Sir Thomas Roe, who was commissioned by various English noblemen to find works of art for their collections, and was introduced to the treasures of Delos by Greek ecclesiastics. The looting of Delos seems to have been a favourite diversion of passing ships. Digby admired a colossal statue of Apollo, in two pieces, which none of them had yet succeeded in removing. Finally its head, arms and feet were said to have been broken off and taken away, by either an English or a Venetian traveller.*

The white houses of Mykonos

The principal neighbour of Delos is Mykonos, an island with no great past, but a spirited present. It is a hump of barren land set in an ultramarine sea and brought vividly to life by the whiteness and brightness of a spontaneous architectural style. Here, in terms of the arts of building and living, is the vernacular idiom of the Cyclades. The craftsmen of Mykonos use their organic materials, the granite and rubble and lime of their native soil, to build their houses and shops and churches, as they have done for centuries past. They do so, however, in no conscious traditionalist spirit, but as seems to them natural, creating instinctively the structural forms,

* These operations are fully described by Terence Spencer in *Fair Greece, Sad Relic* (Weidenfeld & Nicolson, 1954).

the cubes and spheres and cylinders which so blend with the bold contours of their island landscape as to seem an integral element in its formation.

Initially functional, stark and square, their houses are thickly enveloped in layers of plaster, then coats of whitewash renewed so often, in a spirit of cleanliness, that walls and roofs and domes become clothed, as it were, in a new substance, all corners rounded and outlines softened as by icing sugar or a gentle fall of snow.* It is a substance infinitely flexible, as of some pliant form of concrete, achieving naturally, more subtly, and with less angularity, the forms which a Corbusier seeks to achieve by contrivance: forms indeed more daring, as in the use of steps at conflicting angles, in defiance of proportions and even, it seems, of gravity. No standardized formula inhibits the architect, who builds individually, as convenience may move him, but always with an eye to his environment. He thus helps to build up, within the limits of a traditional design, but at different levels and in an elastic variety of heights and sizes, an architectural complex resolving itself into an alive and harmonious whole. Nature completes it, pouring down sunlight and shadow to give an added dramatic emphasis to shapes and forms.

A white-domed chapel protects the harbour, frequented as freely as the taverns and cafés and tourist shops which encircle a waterfront brimming with painted boats.† Paved streets run inland from it and up the hillside, narrow and sociable, shiningly clean with sunlit whitewash, covering the walls and pavements. Balconies cross them, like bridges, life moving across from the sun into the shade, where old women sit chattering over games of cards, and fishermen squat mending long brown nets, spread out over the neat cobbled pavements. Commanding the town from above is a chain of stout windmills, their wide wheels creaking, their white sails flapping in the wind.‡ Billowing above the flat white roofs below, scattered also over the rocky brown slopes of the island in such profusion as to outnumber the pagan shrines of Delos, are the rounded domes and barrel-vaults of churches and chapels and shrines.

Today, however, the sacred centre of the Cyclades is the neighbouring island of Tinos, where the Virgin attracts pilgrims from all the Greek world, as Apollo used to do. Paros draws them, too, to a triple white church in a cloistered garden, fresh with cypresses and flowering shrubs, which has grown in importance, and deteriorated in style, from the simplicity of Byzantium to the flamboyance of the eighteenth century. It was from this island that the Greeks brought the whitest of marble to face the temple of Delphi and the earlier Acropolis – a marble which has been used with bizarre effect to build a fortress tower, its walls composed of a jumble of ancient column drums and lintels.

The cone of Naxos rises beyond it, a Venetian citadel swallowed by a Greek Cycladic town, its medieval walls now whitewashed and pitted with rows of

* Plate, p. 63.   † Plate, p. 70.   ‡ Plate, p. 69.

domestic windows. These islands continued to be ruled by Venetian ducal families until the later part of the sixteenth century. The last Duke of Naxos was finally dethroned by the Turks at the request of the Greek inhabitants themselves, who hoped as a result to enjoy its revenues. But the Turkish Sultan, Selim II, farmed them out to a Portuguese Jew, who encouraged in him a taste for its admirable wines. Once, under their influence, the Sultan went so far as to promise the Jew the still Christian Kingdom of Cyprus, whose wines were better still. Taking him at his word, he assumed the island's armorial bearings, making plans for the replacement of the Greek population by Jews.

All these islands continued, under the Turks, to retain some autonomy. Moreover from time to time one of their more educated citizens was able to gain favour at the Sultan's court, where Greeks grew more and more powerful from the eighteenth century onwards. One such was Mavroyene, a Greek of Mykonos, who became dragoman of the Turkish fleet, and used his influence to improve the situation of his fellow Greeks throughout the Ottoman Empire.

6

Islands to the east

Aegean travel is a picnic. Apart from an occasional liner, on which tourists cruise in stately isolation, the boats which speed in and out of Piraeus, tossing over the seas from one island to another, provide only rudimentary comfort. But they provide life. First-class cabins are few, second-class cabins congested. Service is, at the best, rough and ready. Life is lived on and below decks, where a gregarious crowd reclines amid a confused impedimenta of baskets and bundles, tin trunks and wooden suitcases, wine casks, live poultry and cooking pots. A mule pokes its nose through the window of the saloon; a peasant lets a sheep out of a bag. A sailor strums at an accordion; a soldier twangs at a lute, humming a monotonous chant from the depths of some Byzantine past. A companion rises to dance to it, solitary, slow and sedate.

Greeks thus gathered together are given to drama. On deck in the moonlight men lie wakeful, in shirt sleeves and boots; women sleep shrouded in black, still as corpses. Presently the men, soldiers and sailors and students and peasants, become aware that the bridge, just above them, is peopled with schoolgirls. All faces are turned to it. Sleepers awake. Voices are raised in a mass serenade – snatches of poetry, jests, declarations, floating up over the balmy moonlit air. A sailor impulsively mounts the companion-way, playfully straddles the barrier, strikes the pose of a Romeo. The Juliets scurry away in the darkness, leaving an Amazon to hold the bridge. In a fuss of agitation an officer appears. Stout, spherical, apoplectic, he stumps to the rostrum, half topples over the rails, brandishes fat hands as he harangues the recumbent troupe below.

'These girls are in my charge ... you molest them at your peril ...'

There is a chorus of ribaldry. 'Oh, Officer, have you no heart? ... Up there in the moonlight you have women ... We are men, we are human ... Oh, the balmy night air ... *the temptation!*'

'Come, comrades,' cries one, 'let us fill our shoes with *retsina* and send it up to them.'

In his excitement, himself perhaps yearning a little, the officer stumps from one member of the crew to another. 'You are mobilized,' he warns. 'They outnumber us. They may try to rush the bridge. Stand by for action stations.'

But of a sudden the comedy finishes. The actors are tired of it. Sleep descends on the decks, on a frieze of confused prone figures, serene or grotesque or hieratic in a sequence of sculptural poses.

To the south, as to the north, of the Cyclades lie the islands which the Greeks call the Sporades. Soon after dawn the ship calls at Ios, the home of Homer's mother and perhaps the site of his tomb: the crescent of a bay, the white cubes of a village, the shadowy cone of a mountain materialize slowly through an early morning haze. An hour ahead, crouching darkly on the horizon in the glint of the rising sunlight, tower the more ominous forms of a volcanic creation – the island of Santorin. Between frowning rocks, the ship passes, as it were, into a nether world: a Stygian 'lagoon', blue as ink and still as oil, where a hot mist steams up over scorched and naked cliffs. Ash-red and coal-black, they have caved in and crumbled, leaving a salt-white village encrusted high around their rim – the village of Epanomeria. By the water's edge, above tall precarious jetties, barrel-vaulted hives, dusty and red as the rock, provide dwellings and stores as though for some subterranean species. It is as if the earth had split open, revealing, in section, at two levels, two forms of life.*

An unearthly light descends on the water, giving a sulphurous glow to the boats rowing out, like Charon's ferry, to take passengers off the ship. Voices echo weirdly in the rockbound stillness. A fisherman sells his catch, still flapping in the nets, of outlandish fish, some vividly scarlet, some flat and white with apparent wings. More passengers come on board, black-eyed old women, one thinly bearded, with limbs as gnarled as the branches of an olive tree.

This wide half-moon of ragged cliffs, some eighteen miles in circumference with a satellite island split off to the north of it, is all that remains of Santorin, since the bulk of the island was torn away from it by a volcanic upheaval, vanishing beneath the sea. They are in effect the outer walls of a crater, lying deep in the heart of the lagoon, throwing up through the centuries smaller islands, which survive or disappear in their turn. The initial catastrophe occurred in Mycenean times. Strabo describes a later eruption, at the beginning of the second century B.C., when 'flames rushed forth from the sea for the space of four days; causing the whole of it to boil and be all on fire; and after a little an island twelve stadia in circumference, composed of the burning mass, was thrown up, as if raised by machinery.' An eruption in Byzantine times was widely regarded as an outburst of divine displeasure at the iconoclastic ravages of the Emperor Leo. On this occasion the neighbouring islands

* Plate, p. 80.

were enveloped in vapour and smoke, while dust and pumice, showered over the sea, were carried as far as the coasts of Macedonia and Asia Minor. An eruption of the seventeenth century threw up an island which soon afterwards subsided, to become a submarine reef. Tournefort, the eighteenth-century botanist, expresses amazement at all these islands risen from the bottom of the sea. 'What a frightful sight to see the teeming Earth bring forth such unwieldy Burdens! What prodigious Force must there needs be, to move them, displace them, and lift them above the water!...What shocks, what concussions...!'

The eruption of 1925 heaved most of them together into a single island, where lava and pumice have solidified to make an amorphous heap of rock, still sporadically smoking – a black star in the centre of the red crescent.* Opposite lies the principal port of the island. Devoid of an anchorage, from the unfathomable depth of the sea, it huddles at the base of a steep cliff of tufa, spongy as gingerbread, corrugated as with pillars and pitted with troglodyte dwellings. Stratified rocks tower above it: layers, as it were, of a dead planet, interposed between the sea and a town which has survived above, straggling loosely along the skyline and sprawling carelessly over it, to poise buildings as though on the brink of an abyss. A cobbled path zigzags seven hundred feet up, over the pulverized slope, around russet-brown crags and across screes of a yellowish shale. In the windless air and ruthless sunlight, the ascent is a laborious penance. At the head of it the traveller stands marooned high and dry, at the mercy of a white town tumbling around him in a Vorticist warren of streets and stairways, domes and rooftops, all blindingly lit by the sun.†

The classical name of Santorin is Thera, hence that of its capital, Phira. The name Santorin is derived from St Irene, the island's patron saint. It dates from the days of the Latin occupation – days prolonged in spirit throughout the Turkish period, when the Catholics survived in strength, and indeed into Greek times, through the survival of a number of old Latin families. Today Phira still echoes with church bells. But the Catholics are numbered: since the Second World War, in which the Italians were involved, only a few hundreds remain. Their imposing cathedral has a sparse congregation; their convent is almost empty of nuns. The town of Phira, confined to the long sharp spine of the island, prolongs itself interminably along two narrow streets, with never the chance to open out into a square or *piazza*. Waterless, it survives only on rainfall, drawing on a labyrinth of cisterns, often the fruit of benefactions from its wealthier emigrant citizens. Treeless, it relaxes only with darkness. By day the sea, far below, is a dull sheet of ground glass, the black crater island a stain in its centre. By night it relents, transmuted into silver by the light of the moon.

* Serious destruction was caused, here and throughout the island, by a further eruption in 1956.

† Plate, p. 79.

But there is a landward side to Santorin. To the east the ridge falls away into a more distant sea, over a landscape, treeless still and strewn with pumice, but softened as with a textile by the greenery of vines and tomatoes. The wines, with their own tart flavour, the tomato pastes, sweeter than those of the West, relieve an island economy otherwise limited to pumice and china clay. Scattered among the vines is a profusion of white-domed chapels. Rising above them is the island's highest peak, crowned with the monastery of the Prophet Elias. The classical city of Thera lies spread over the opposite slope.

Originally a Dorian settlement, its inhabitants were instructed by the oracle at Delphi to found a city in Libya. The King, declaring himself too old for the task, delegated it to Battus, a younger man, who did not know where Libya was and accordingly took no action. In seven years, according to Herodotus, not a drop of rain fell in Thera, and all but one of its trees were killed by the drought. The Thereans, appealing to Delphi, received a reproachful reminder that they had never colonized Libya. So they sent to Crete, to discover where Libya was, and after landing on an island off its coast, finally founded the city of Cyrene. While building it Battus found an unexpected cure for an impediment in his speech, which Pausanias faithfully records: 'As he was travelling in the remote parts of Cyrene which were still unoccupied, he chanced to see a lion, and his terror at the sight made him cry out loud and clearly.'

The ruins of Thera, a city well-built from the local basalt, date largely from the Ptolemaic period, and contain shrines to Egyptian as well as Greek gods. Nearby are the relics of elegant Ptolemaic houses, one carved with a phallus, and an inscription which offers hospitality 'to the friends of our friends'. There is a shrine dedicated to an admiral of the Ptolemies, Artemidorus, his effigy carved on the naked rock together with the profiles of the Eagle of Zeus, the Lion of Apollo and the Dolphin of Poseidon. There is a terrace with Dorian foundations, where, after the manner of Sparta, youths danced naked in honour of their national Apollo, moreover carved their names on the rocks, among those of the gods. There is a large gymnasium, with cubicles for the youths of a later period, and a small Roman theatre, in which a cistern was built beneath the seats, to collect any rainwater which fell on the auditorium.

Directly below the precipitous city lies the village of Perissa, its many-domed white church contrasting dramatically with a black volcanic beach. Here the shingle shelves down to a sea so deep that it is possible to dive into it straight from the sand. The sun gives a silvery glint to the stony flanks of the mountain, and an emerald glow to the vines, criss-crossed at its feet. The surrounding villages of the plain are poor and often sombre places. They owe much, however, to the philanthropy of their own people who migrate to earn their living in Athens. A rich shipowner

SEVEN HUNDRED FEET UP FROM THE SEA stands Phira, the capital of Santorin – a
warren of streets and stairways, white domes and rooftops, all blindingly lit by the sun.

has supplied his native island with a road and tourist hotel. Other villagers form societies in Athens, to which each contributes, rich or poor, according to his means. Each year they will come home to the island in hundreds to celebrate the feast of some local patron saint.

Then, for a few days and nights, life is a holiday. The white houses are decked with flags and garlands. The square is packed with tables, at which families eat and drink and talk and sing – villagers in cloth caps, Athenians in panamas, girls in their party frocks. As dusk falls musical instruments emerge, and soon they are dancing, in a pandemonium of sound, to the discord of three competitive orchestras.

Rhodes: city of the Knights

The southern Sporades lie, for the most part, strung along the coasts of Asia Minor. They embrace the Dodecanese, the group of twelve islands so named, for administrative reasons, in Byzantine times. Chief among them is the large island of Rhodes, lying in the lee of the south-westerly headland of Turkey. Rhodes is the home of Helios, the Sun God. He left it to Rhodon, his favourite nymph, and it was peopled by their children, the Heliades.

The island has a key geographical position, to which it owes a distinguished history. The Minoans of Crete made it their first easterly outpost, facilitating the colonization of the coasts and islands of Asia Minor. Later it became a Dorian settlement, playing the dominant part in a league of six Greek cities, founded in defence against the natives of the mainland, and expanding to found colonies of its own, as far east as Cilicia, as far west as Sicily and Spain. Thus the Rhodians built up a commercial empire, which rivalled that of Athens and flourished for many centuries. After the death of Alexander it won and maintained its independence, extending its influence more widely, not only in the commercial but in the political field. In Roman times it prospered greatly, enjoying free access to the mainland, and some administrative control of it, and the population rose to half a million. The Rhodian Navy was of considerable use to Pompey in his operations against the pirates and against Julius Caesar.

Bestriding, or at least commanding, the harbour of Rhodes was the famous Colossus, one of the seven wonders of the classical world. A memorial of the Rhodian war of independence, against the successors of Alexander, it was a statue of Helios the Sun God, a hundred and five feet high, which took twelve years to cast. Its fingers were each said to be as large as any ordinary statue. It was destroyed in an earthquake after only fifty-six years, but survived in ruins, an imposing mass of rock and iron, for nine hundred years more. Finally, in Saracen times, it was sold as scrap to a Jewish contractor, who used nine hundred – or more likely ninety – camels to carry it away.

ORCHED AND NAKED CLIFFS with the salt-white village of Epanomeria crusted around their rim. Below, the wharves and storehouses of Phira.

The colossal scale prevailed at Rhodes. Demetrius, himself described as a second Alexander, who tried to subdue the city for his father Antigonus, brought against it a mammoth siege engine, named the Helepolis: a moving tower on wheels of oak, nine stories high and seventy-five feet broad, which needed three thousand four hundred men to propel it. Complete with catapults, battering rams and draw-bridges, a top floor which was a nest for archers, and a lower floor with water tanks, serviced by pumps and hoses made from the intestines of cattle, it overtopped the Rhodian walls, but failed to secure the victory. When an honourable peace was finally made, Demetrius ceded his war material to the Rhodians, and it was on the proceeds of the sale of this that the Colossus was erected.

Little remains of classical Rhodes save the layout of two of its artificial harbours, of which a series of five were built of a fine local stone, in the finished style of the Hellenistic period. But an unfamiliar civilization has descended upon them. The imposing spectacle which greets the traveller, as his ship sails into the Grand Harbour of Rhodes today, is that of a medieval city: walls and bastions of a weathered golden stone, enfolding the anchorage in an austere embrace; the battlements and towers of a feudal castle frowning aggressively above them. For Rhodes gained a new lease of life with the Crusades. Driven from Palestine at the end of the thirteenth century, the Knights of St John of Jerusalem captured the island from the Byzantines, converted it into a fortress, and held it for more than two centuries, with fortified outposts on the island of Kos, and on the mainland, at Halicarnassus.

They thrived on the business of pilgrimage, which had survived the fall of the Holy Places into Moslem hands, exploited the island's commercial resources, plundered Turkish shipping, and became, with the Venetians on the one hand and the Genoese on the other, a key power in the Frankish control of Greek waters. They resisted the Turks with success in two sieges no less dramatic than that of Demetrius, but eventually succumbed to them and were allowed to depart with their arms and property, withdrawing in succession to Crete, to Tripoli and to their ultimate home on the island of Malta.

The rock-cut, stone-built moat of their fortress recalls that of Valletta, at Malta. Descending to a depth of seventy feet, it encircles two and a half miles of ramparts, the severity of their stone now softened with lichens and mosses, wild flowers and blossoming fruit trees. As broad as a street, they command a view of the roofs of the city and of the blue sea spread beneath it. Crusaders of all nations – England, Germany, Italy, Spain, France – kept guard over these walls, each with its own allotted section of bastions and sentry points. The gates and streets and towers still recall them: Angleterre Street, Auvergne Street, Aragon Street, Provence Street; Naillac's Tower, the Amboise Gate, the Towers of Spain and Italy. In the steep cobbled Street of the Knights, like some alley in a French medieval town, are their inns and lodges, graced with armorial bearings. Stern in their stone façades, they are relieved with leafy, flowery courtyards behind their studded doorways.

Above all towers the palace of the Grand Masters, elaborately restored by the Italians as the seat of a Fascist Governor-General. For Italy captured the Dodecanese islands in 1912, and ruled over them for a generation, ceding them to Greece at the end of the Second World War. Below lies the cloistered infirmary of the Knights, who were Hospitallers by function. Built in the Gothic style and restored by the Italians, with wards like aisles and a sanctuary so placed that the patients might join in services without leaving their beds, it is now a museum, containing relics of classical Rhodes, among them a Venus raised from the bottom of the harbour, her features worn and encrusted through the ages by the action of the sea.

Some of the churches of Rhodes lie in ruins – Gothic ruins, their grey stone seasoned and gilded by the Eastern Mediterranean sunlight. Others were turned into mosques by the Turks. The infidel town still survives within the Christian walls, its slender minarets rising incongruously above the rugged feudal battlements. It is a warren of narrow winding streets, of house fronts plastered and brightly painted, of zigzag stairways with treads washed blue, bow windows and balconies craning forwards as though to meet one another across the street. Here and there they make way for a haphazard square, with a mosque and a fountain in the centre. Greeks and Turks, living in harmony, give a polyglot air to the city, reflecting, under Greek rule, an atmosphere which prevailed throughout the coastlands of Turkey before the expulsion by the Turks of the Greek population after the First World War. The mixture is leavened still further by a sprinkling of Italians, who remained behind after the second.

In the evenings Greek and Turkish music blares from the radios in the cafés. Beneath the moonlit battlements, by the Italian Tower of the Knights, is a humble Greek café, with walls of flaking plaster and an uneven pavement of pebble mosaic. Here, under the glare of an acetylene lamp, within a circle of tables at which men drink *retsina*, a young boy in shorts dances alone, with all the solemnity of innocence, in a slow sedate Greek rhythm. A sailor claps for him in time to the loudspeaker's music. A cook fans the embers of a charcoal brazier, grilling meat on spits for the men who sit watching him. A boy on a bicycle, a man on an Italian motor scooter, stop to watch. A bus goes by, its passengers all turning to see what is happening. Around rise tenements with lighted windows, insubstantial as stage scenery against the backcloth of medieval walls. Flowers bloom in whitewashed petrol tins; a canary perches in a cage on a window sill. At the windows, on stairways, at doorsteps, families squat, gazing downwards, relieved by the cool of the night. Children wrestle in the dust; a baby sleeps in a hammock; a woman sweeps out a room, giving on to the pavement, where a man lies ill, perhaps dying. The dance finishes. The dancer picks up his basket of peanuts and hawks them among the crowd. Then he goes on his way.

Outside the walls, to the north, by the harbour of Mandraki which the sailors of the classical galleys called the Sheepfold, the Italians have built a bright modern quarter, in the *opéra comique* manner. Among gardens of pink oleander, hedged in by scarlet hibiscus, looking across to a mole where a line of red-roofed windmills marches out towards the lighthouse and the Fort of St Nicholas, is a seafront colonnaded in the Italian style, with cafés and shops beneath the archways; a modern church built by the Knights of St John; a Palace of Justice and government offices, built in the style of the Doges' Palace at Venice. At the point of the island, at the base of a white spit of sand, pointing out across the sound towards the Turkish coast and the blue peaks of the Taurus above it, they have built, where the Colossus may once have stood, an imposing luxury hotel, with a beach of its own.

Rhodes itself was but one of the four Greek cities on the island, and indeed later in date than the others – Kamiros in its valley, Jalysos on its mountain, Lindos on its glittering bay. For it was founded, in the fifth century B.C., to unite their resources into a single capital, aspiring thus to compete with Athens and Sparta. The cities, or at least their sites, are linked by roads which encircle the mountainous core of the island. They wind through an undulating dry Greek landscape, shaded by olives and cypresses, scattered with villages of flat-roofed houses, white cubes shining in the sun. The mountains assume gay fantastic shapes as they prance down to the sea, breaking the coast into an infinity of coves and inlets, fringed by smooth white beaches. Here, commanding natural twin harbours, is Lindos, the second city of the island.

Classical Lindos has not been engulfed, like Rhodes, by the fortifications of the Knights. On the contrary, they protect it, in a rough and incongruous embrace. Perched on a black nugget of rock, dropping sheer to the sea, are the sun-gilt towers of another Crusader castle. Within its battlements, relics of a rude medieval strife, stand the slender columns of a Doric temple, built a thousand years earlier in a more graceful, if not always a more serene age.* Beneath them a steep white town, red-roofed and pebble-paved, piles itself up to the walls of the fortress, the nave of its white church glowing with murals, black, red and gold, in the Orthodox style. Here, all busy and alive, are the Greeks of today, some living in the decorated houses of the Crusaders, some working still to make the Rhodian pottery, famous since medieval times.

Revelation on Patmos

A tub of a boat, without cabins, plies between Rhodes and the other Dodecanese islands, which lie like a chain around the jutting promontories of south-western

* Plate, p. 86.

A STREET IN RHODES, insubstantial as stage scenery against the backcloth of haphazard growth. Rhodes was the headquarters of the Knights of St John in the middle ages.

Turkey. Close to the shore, in the gulf to which it has given its name, is Simi, where the Persian fleet spent the winter, licking its wounds, after the Battle of Salamis, and where later, ironically, the Athenian victor, Themistocles, first landed when driven into exile by his people. An island of sponge fishers, it has an enclosed rectangular harbour and a town built up in orderly formation, over a treeless hillside, the houses and stairways washed ochre and blue as though to tone respectively with land and sea.

Opposite Simi, to the north, lies the Turkish promontory of Knidos, famous in classical times as a place of pilgrimage, whose attraction was the flawless nude Aphrodite, a masterpiece of Praxiteles. Until a generation ago the people of Simi had lands here, enabling them to relieve an otherwise hard existence. But today a curtain has descended between islands and mainland, and the Greeks of Simi are for ever in trouble for fishing in Turkish waters.

Around Knidos the long tail of the island of Kos coils up to a rugged conical head. More fertile than the rest, it was a classical spa; among rough Byzantine walls and graceful Italian arcades, it still boasts a gigantic plane tree, claimed to have sheltered Hippocrates, the father of medicine, as he dispensed his healing wares.

Kalimnos, like Simi, is an island of sponge fishers – fishers also, unwittingly, of classical statuary, wrecked off these treacherous headlands and raised from the bed of the sea. When the island surrendered to the Turks, it sent the Sultan a tribute of sponges and loaves, especially white since the sponge diver used not to grow corn, but to buy the best flour from his Greek neighbours on the mainland. His operations extend southwards to the coast of Libya, and even farther afield to South America, the Bahamas and Florida, where colonies of Simiots and Kalimniots live today.

Leros, the next port of call, is an island with deep twin harbours, and has thus played the role, through its history, of a major naval base. The Greeks used it as such during the Ionian revolt against the Persians; the Knights, for their operations against the Turks; the Italians, during the Second World War. Today their installations lie derelict, a mass of ignoble concrete ruins. But the Greeks carry on the tradition with a college, to train cadets.

Finally the boat sails into the harbour of Patmos, the white cubes of its houses grouped cleanly around the edge of a land-locked bay. Above them the land slopes steeply up over a brown terraced hillside, to a companion village, which, from far out at sea, gleams like a snow-cap on the horizon.* Soaring boldly over its rooftops, built of a contrasting grey volcanic stone, are the walls and bastions, streamlined and smooth, of an apparent medieval fortress. This is in fact the Monastery of St John the Divine. For it was to Patmos that the Evangelist came, as a refugee from Roman persecution, having survived immersion in a cauldron of boiling oil; and it was here that he received the Revelation, inspiring him to write the Apocalypse.

* Plate, p. 91.

HE CRUSADER CASTLE OF LINDOS preserves within its sun-gilt battlements the slender columns of a Doric temple, built a thousand years earlier in
more graceful, if not a more serene, age.

The monastery was founded in the eleventh century on the site of a temple of Artemis, by a monk called Christodoulos. The son of wealthy parents, he had in a vision spent a night in council with the Apostles, and thereafter reacted against the luxury and corruption of the monasteries of his period to found this more austere establishment of his own. 'Some islands', he remarked, 'have a fertile soil and are too beautiful for an austere life; sterile and dreary Patmos, with all its barrenness, is the place for the strict rules I wish observed.'

Nevertheless he obtained from the Emperor a title deed to richer lands, not merely in Patmos but in the neighbouring islands, in Samos, and as far afield as Crete, of which his monastery still enjoys the revenues. It is a whitewashed labyrinth of courts and stairways, cupolas and rooftops, at a bewildering variety of levels. Within its walls are a number of small chapels, and a Church of St John, giving on to a courtyard deep as a well, where the monks tend pots of richly-flowering plants. The pride of the monastery is its library, whose principal treasure is a manuscript of the Gospel of St Mark – all that remains here of a book, of which other leaves are to be found in the Vatican, in Vienna, and in the British Museum in London.

Beneath the monastery, enclosed by a number of sacred buildings, is the cave where the Evangelist is said to have lodged and to have beheld the Revelation. Converted into a chapel, at the foot of a steep narrow passage, its bluff of overhanging rock has been supported, superfluously, by columns. Beneath it is the stone where the Evangelist's head is believed, by the monks, to have rested, the crevice where he placed his hand while raising himself to pray, even the cleft in the rock through which the great voice of the Holy Ghost, 'as of a trumpet', reached him, revealing the vision of the seven stars and seven golden candlesticks. Spread at the feet of his refuge, sprinkled now with a profusion of white chapels, the dry brown landscape rolls away, a convolution of isthmuses locking the sea in a sinuous rocky embrace. Beyond, like a shadow, Samos rises; beyond that again the more mountainous forms of the Asiatic continent. Here lie those Seven Churches of Asia which received the Evangelist's message. Here too lie the cities of those Ionian colonists, who brought the earlier, earthier, message of classical Greece.

7

Shrines of Olympia and Delphi

Classical Greece looked geographically eastwards, turning its back on the West. The Saronic Gulf throws out its arms wide open to the East, source of the earliest civilizations. The Gulf of Corinth, by comparison, was a mere cleft, dividing the land mass of Greece into two parts, but blocked from the East by an isthmus, thus admitting to it the influences only of the more backward West.

From earliest times attempts were made to transform the Gulf into a thorough-fare, linking the eastern and western seas by breaking through the isthmus. Periander, the dictator of Corinth and one of the Seven Sages of Greece, made plans for a canal as early as the seventh century B.C., inspired by the irrigation engineering achievements of his allies the Egyptians. But, lacking the slave labour resources available to an Egyptian despot, he was unable to carry them out. Demetrius, one of the successors of Alexander, revived the project, but was discouraged, says Strabo, by a report from his engineers that the two seas were on different levels, 'so that if he cut through the isthmus, not only the coasts near Aegina, but even Aegina itself, with the neighbouring islands, would be laid completely under water, while the passage would prove of little value'. This bore out the theory of Eratosthenes, which Strabo scorns, that the Mediterranean, though one entire sea, had 'not the same level, even at points quite close to each other'.

The Romans, under Julius Caesar and Caligula, were the next to consider the enterprise. Nero, for the first time, actually tried to carry it out, employing a labour force of Jewish prisoners whom he sought to encourage by digging in person, with a golden shovel. But neither this nor any other attempt succeeded owing, as Pausanias hints, to divine obstruction: 'Whoever attempted to make the Peloponnese an island died before the completion of a canal across the isthmus.' So the Greeks continued laboriously to drag their lighter shipping by machinery overland.

The canal, based on a plan similar to Nero's, was finally undertaken by French

and completed by Greek contractors, towards the end of the nineteenth century. A
street, as it were, of water, just broad enough for a single ship, it has walls rising
steeply on either side, their geological strata, cut with steps and reinforced with
masonry, recalling the various archaeological levels of some prehistoric city. Curi-
ously enough a trick of perspective gives the illusion, which would please Erastos-
thenes, that the canal is sloping uphill, from one gulf to the other.

Corinth itself lies to the south of the canal, protected by the towering mountain
fortress of the Acrocorinth, crowned once with a temple of Aphrodite, now with a
Venetian castle. Endowed with ports on the two seas and commanding the land
route from one to another, it was a city which shook itself free of the domination of
Argos to become an important commercial state, helping to civilize the West with
its own colonies, notably Corcyra (Corfu) and Syracuse. Hardly a serious rival of
Athens, Corinth nevertheless played a key part in maintaining the balance of power
between Athens and Sparta, throwing her weight first on one side, then on the
other, and finally precipitating the Peloponnesian War as Sparta's ally.

Not only trade but sports meetings and religious festivals drew quantities of
visitors to the city, where some found an especial attraction in the thousand courte-
sans, dedicated to the service of the temple of Aphrodite. It was a city noted for the
arts of painting and sculpture, notably in bronze, hence was plundered with peculiar
rapacity by the Romans: the Corinthians had insulted them by throwing down filth
from their windows on the heads of the Roman ambassadors. The ignorant Roman
soldiery flung a painting by Polygnotos on the ground to play dice on; their
General, with more discrimination, carried away a quantity of paintings and
statuary to embellish Rome and the neighbouring cities; but he too was so ignorant
of the arts as to decree that, if any of the treasures were lost in transport, they must
be replaced by those responsible. The population was exterminated and the city remained deserted for a century. It was then repopulated by Julius Caesar, with
Roman colonists, who found more treasures – notably vases from the tombs. These
fetched big prices in Rome where, as Necro-Corinthia, they were fashionable for a
time.

The city whose ruins now lie spread at the foot of the Acrocorinth is largely
Roman in period. But the columns of a Doric temple of Apollo survive, high above
the Gulf, somewhat thick in dimensions and of an eroded pinkish stone. The city
was well supplied with water, by two interconnected springs known as the Pierene,
one at the summit and one at the foot of the mountain. It was here that the winged
horse Pegasus was drinking when Bellerophon captured and harnessed him with a
golden bridle. Water still bubbles up from the spring, behind an elegant colonnade
with which the Romans adorned it, while its overflow fills a rectangular Roman
basin. It is, as the inveterate tourist Pausanias wrote, 'beautified with white stone,

GLEAMING LIKE A SNOW-CAPPED HILL from far out to sea, Patmos slopes steeply up to a white village. The monastery soars boldly above. On this spot, St John received the Revelation.

and there are cells like caves to match, from which the water trickles into that part of the well which is in the open air, and it has a sweet taste, and they say that Corinthian brass when hissing hot is dipped into this water'. In various parts of the city, with its broad paved streets, are the remains of other wells and fountains, together with traces of a system of running water which served the shops and taverns.

The Panhellenic Festival

The Gulf of Corinth runs on like a gleaming fjord between the mountains of the Peloponnese and the mountains of central Greece. Its western outlet is guarded by the port of Patras, ally of Athens when Corinth, its eastern complement, was the ally of Sparta. Its citadel has survived a chequered history, in the course of which it was held for some time by the Pope. The town now lying at its feet is a product of the Greek War of Independence, built in an arcaded style more Italian than Greek, by Capo d'Istria, the Corfiote of Italian origin who served successively imperial Russia as a diplomat and republican Greece as president.

From Patras a broad plain spreads southward, between the mountains and the sea, then inland up the broad and fertile valley of the Alpheos River to the point where it joins the Kladeos. By this easy route, from the Heroic Age onwards, came migrant Greek tribes from the north, beyond the Gulf of Corinth; and on the banks of this river they settled to found, in the name of Zeus, their northern God, the city of Olympia. Serving as a link between the Greeks of East and West, of North and South, it was destined to become one of the international centres of the Hellenic world.

The impulse towards unity, among the diverse tribes of Greeks, began to grow with the advance of colonization. Contact with the barbarians beyond the seas emphasized their sense of Greekness, and led them into closer relations with Greeks of other cities. They began to see themselves as members of a common Hellenic race, with a common history, common gods and common interests, and to seek an outlet for this feeling in some concrete Panhellenic sense. This was to find expression in terms, not explicitly of politics, but in the first place of religion and in the second of sport. Two major Panhellenic festival centres thus developed – one at Olympia, the other at Delphi.

At Olympia the emphasis was predominantly on sport – though religion was inseparable from it. The Olympic Games – indeed organized games as a whole – had their origins in heroic times. Traditionally they were founded by Hercules, to celebrate his victory over Augeas who had failed to reward him for cleansing his stables by diverting the rivers Alpheos and Peneios through them. Gathering together his armies and their booty, he 'measured a sacred grove for his sovereign father Zeus'.

GARGANTUAN DRUMS OF FALLEN COLUMNS lie scattered among the wild flowers – or lifted on to a rough plinth as a memorial – where once stood the great temple of Zeus at Olympia.

Pindar continues: 'Having fenced round the Altis, he marked the bounds thereof in a clear space, and the plain encompassing it he ordained for rest and feasting.' Then 'he set apart the choicest of the spoil for an offering from the war and sacrificed, and he ordained the fifth year feast with the first Olympiad and prizes of victory.'

Historically the games were founded – or revived – in the eighth century, to celebrate not a victory but a truce between the two local monarchs of Elis and Pisa. The area was neutralized; moreover a general truce prevailed during the period when competitors were travelling to and from the games. Gradually they became an international event, in which first Sparta, then the other Greek states participated; more especially they brought together, in the mother country, citizens of the eastern and western colonies, enabling them to make contact and exchange ideas with their mainland countrymen, and thus fostering a spirit of national unity.

Olympia lies at the foot of the Arcadian highlands, in a soft and fertile landscape. Its two rivers, with their clean white gravel beds, nourish green fields and orchards and groves of cypress, converting the land, as it were, into a garden. Mount Kronion, dedicated successively to Kronos and Zeus, is wooded today with fragrant pines, which spread also over the broad level site of the Altis, the sacred city beneath it. This was dominated by the temple of Olympian Zeus, as indeed it is still by its great long base, though only the stumps of its Doric columns remain. Brought down by an earthquake, in Byzantine times, their gargantuan drums, of eroded grey limestone, lie staggered as they fell, or scattered farther afield among the wild flowers and weeds of a tangled, scented 'park'.*

Large as it seems, the temple was nevertheless dwarfed by the statue of Zeus, the work of Phidias, within it. Carved from ivory and gold, it was a six times life-size figure, reaching almost to the roof, moreover seated, hence presenting the appearance, as Strabo remarks, 'that, if it should rise and stand upright, it would unroof the temple': an anomaly of proportion between sculpture and architecture common to most Greek temples, and due presumably to the demands of religion. The figure grasped in one hand an image of victory, and in the other a sceptre, adorned with precious stones and surmounted by an eagle. Its robes and sandals were of gold, the robes being painted with flowers and the throne itself with beasts by Panaenos, a nephew of Phidias, who painted a number of other pictures for the enclosure in which the statue stood. In front of it was a pavement of black stone; for the ivory in the statue was cleaned with oil, to preserve it from the damp of the Sacred Grove.

The pediments and frieze of the temple, now in the Olympia museum, may also be his work. Representing Olympian contests – Zeus presiding over a chariot race, Apollo taming the Centaurs, Hercules performing his labours – they took fifteen years to complete, and in their vitality and poetry and faultless composition, rank among the masterpieces of classical sculpture. Here also, in the style of its later age,

* Plate, p. 92.

more human than divine, more like a modern ideal of male beauty, is the Hermes of Praxiteles. It came, as it happens, from an earlier temple, whose walls were of mud brick, with columns of wood, and thus in falling preserved it.

Sacrifices to Zeus were performed at a Grand Altar, twenty-two feet high, of which the site may still be seen. It was composed of the débris of the thigh bones of the victims, their ashes collected once a year and kneaded with the waters of the Alpheos. Only the wood of the white poplar tree, imported by Hercules, was used in the sacrifices. The kites, though birds of prey, normally did not interfere with them; if they did touch the flesh or entrails of a victim, it was a bad omen for the sacrificer.

Innumerable shrines and statues and offerings used to crowd the sacred enclosure of Altis, where now, beneath the pine trees, lie only a profusion of stones, with the relics of walls and foundations and an occasional standing column. The temple of Hera may be traced, a goddess who had games of her own, with races for maidens of various ages, and sixteen matrons to weave her a shawl. Pausanias was told by his guide that when the Romans restored the temple they found, between the roof and the ceiling, the body of a dead man in heavy armour: the victim of a battle between Elis and Sparta, some centuries earlier, who had taken refuge there and died of his wounds. Beyond, on a terrace beneath the hillside, are the ruins of the treasuries, chapels, as it were, built by the various Greek cities to house their offerings left after the Games. It is significant that half of them were dedicated by colonies overseas, whose athletes, by the sixth century, were competing hotly with those of the mother country.

The cities tended to vie with one another in the size of the statues of Zeus which they presented to the god, and which were disposed around the sacred precincts. They varied from ten foot to twenty-seven foot high. Often they were erected by the people of Elis themselves, from the proceeds of the fines imposed on competitors for foul play and similar misdemeanours. Bribery and other such forms of cheating at boxing, wrestling or athletics were thus punished and immortalized. A Greek boxer from Alexandria was fined because, on being disqualified for arriving late, he rushed at the winner and attacked him. Before one statue of Zeus it was the custom for athletes, together with their fathers, brothers and trainers, to swear over the entrails of a boar that they would not cheat at the games.

Other statues were effigies of competitors themselves. There were those, in bronze, of the thirty-five choir boys, with their choir master and piper, from Sicily, who were drowned in a storm in the Straits of Messina, on their way to the games. There was the bronze horse with its charioteer, an animal so fashioned that, according to Pausanias, 'stallions not only in spring but all the year round are madly in lust after it. For they rush into Altis, breaking their reins or escaping from their drivers, and endeavour to mount this horse, with far greater impetuosity than they exhibit to the handsomest mare alive whom they had been accustomed to mount. And though their hoofs slip on the polished basement, they do not cease to neigh fiercely, and to try to mount this horse with frantic energy, till by whips or sheer strength they get pulled off.'

There was the statue of Leontiscus, a Sicilian wrestler who 'was not an adept at wrestling his antagonists down, but he used to beat them by trying to break their fingers'. There was Polydamus, the strong man who emulated Hercules by killing a lion on Mount Olympus, and who once 'approached a herd of cattle, and seized the strongest and wildest bull by one of its hind feet, and held on fast by its hoofs, and would not let it go though it kicked and struggled, till at last the bull exerting all its strength got away from him and left its hoof in his hands.' Another strong man, named Milo, tied a cord round his forehead, as if it were a fillet or a crown, and holding his breath and filling the veins of his head with blood he would snap the cord by the strength of his veins. There was the runner Dromeus, who introduced a training diet of meat, whereas athletes had previously eaten 'only a particular kind of cheese'; the boxer Damarchus, who was believed to have changed from a man into a wolf and back again, ten years later; Pantarces, 'who beat all the boys in wrestling, and was beloved by Phidias'; and Theagenes, who had won fourteen hundred prizes, and whose statue was scourged every night by an enemy, but fell on him, was indicted for murder, and thrown into the sea. Finally, after a period of drought, it was retrieved by fishermen following a recommendation from the oracle at Delphi. Visiting athletes put the finishing touches to their training in the gymnasium and its *palestra*, to the west of the sacred precincts, whose ruins survive. The *palestra* had a large courtyard in the centre, which was strewn with sand for the benefit of wrestlers. Around it was a covered colonnade, which may have served as a running track. Its rooms included an undressing room, a large clubroom, a bathroom with a large sunken tank (but no hot water as in the more luxurious Roman baths), rooms with benches from which visitors could watch the athletes, and storerooms for athletic apparatus and for oil, with which the athletes rubbed themselves, afterwards powdering themselves, before exercise – a practice, together with that of stripping naked for athletics, which was started by the Spartans.

The contests themselves took place in a stadium, with a two-hundred-yard course, beyond the eastern walls of the Altis, which was said to have been stepped out by Hercules in person. Reached by a broad tunnelled passage, its starting and finishing lines can still be seen: sockets for posts and grooves for a toe-grip, cut into narrow slabs of pavement. The racecourse, which lay near to it, has been carried away by the river.

The original programme of events consisted of the foot race, from a two-

hundred-yard sprint to a three-mile run; the chariot race, first for two-horse, later
for four-horse chariots, with large fields, over a course of nine miles with up to
twenty-three turns, involving frequent accidents; throwing the *diskos*, a plate of
metal or stone which weighed from three to fifteen pounds; throwing the javelin,
a light pole, the height of a man, with a leather throwing-thong attached; boxing,
with blows only at the head, not the body, at first with soft, then with harder
leather thongs, tied around the hands, and finally, in Roman times, with the savage
addition of metal and even spikes; finally wrestling of two kinds, one designed
merely to throw, the other continuing after the throw, on the ground, which was
usually watered until it grew muddy, making the body hard to hold and moreover
benefiting the skin. Later the *pankration* was introduced, a form of all-in wrestling
in which strangling, arm-twisting, hitting, kicking and jumping on an opponent –
indeed all but biting him or gouging out his eyes – were allowed. Finally there was
the *pentathlon*, a combination of five events designed to combat professionalism and
encourage the all-round athlete, calling for qualities not merely of brawn but of
brain and indeed also of beauty.

All this was done not for a prize of money but for a crown of wild olive leaves,
plucked from a tree behind the temple. When the Persians, before Salamis, were told
this, one of them 'could not help crying out in front of everybody, "Good heavens,
Mardonius, what kind of men are these that you have brought us to fight against –
men who compete with one another for no material reward, but only for honour!"'
It was a remark, notes Herodotus, 'which proved his true nobility of character –
though it made Xerxes call him a coward'. In fact there were richer prizes for the
winners, when they returned home to their native cities.

Indirectly there were prizes too, of a political character, for the rulers and
politicians who used their proficiency at the games as a means of gaining prestige
and power. Alcibiades, for example, won honour and glory, both popular and
international, by entering the record number of seven four-horse chariots for a race,
and carrying off the first, second and fourth prizes. After Salamis, when Themistocles appeared on the racecourse, 'all the spectators took no further interest in the
contests, but passed the whole day in admiring and applauding him ... so that he was
delighted, and said to his friends that he had now received his reward for all his
labours on behalf of Greece.'

In the following century, when Greece had relapsed once more into disunity,
Olympia became on three notable occasions a platform for statesmen pleading for
an active Panhellenic union. For Persia, in unholy alliance with Sparta, was once
more a menace. They did not succeed. Only the last, the Athenian Isocrates, was to
see his project of union realized – not through free association, but through the sub-
mission of all Greece to a single sovereign, Philip of Macedon. It enabled him to die

happy while Demosthenes, the diehard nationalist, mourned, bent as he was on uniting the Greeks against 'the Macedonian wretch'. Isocrates, with his broader perception, had divined that only under Macedon could the Asiatic menace be finally dispelled, and Greek civilization expand eastwards as it should. Philip himself ran his horses at Olympia, and won a race there on the day that Alexander was born – a sure omen of his invincibility. He started to build an elegant rotunda, in the Ionic manner, which Alexander completed. Its ruins still survive.

The Romans first plundered Olympia, then embellished it in their own more sumptuous manner, while Nero introduced competitions for musicians, poets and dramatists. The last Olympiad was held at the end of the fourth century A.D., already in the Christian era. The last recorded victor was an Armenian who, in order to compete, was obliged to prove his Hellenic descent, but was probably in fact more proud of his Romaic citizenship. The great statue of Zeus was removed to Constantinople, where it was later destroyed in a fire. The other statue by Phidias, representing Minerva, was removed at about the same time, so that no authentic work of his now survives. The temple was destroyed not long after, either by Alaric's Goths or by bigoted Christians, their work being finished off by earthquakes.

The lap of the gods

When Philip of Macedon advanced southwards into the Peloponnese, he took care to secure the Gulf of Corinth by the capture of Navpaktos, the port on the north shore which commands the narrows – 'the little Dardanelles'. Traditionally it was here, 'the place of the ship building', that the Dorians, moving similarly southward some thousand years earlier, stopped to build themselves a fleet. Aware of the strategic importance of Navpaktos, Athens seized it well in advance of the Peloponnesian War, settled it with discontented subjects of Sparta, and fought three major naval engagements to hold it. In the sixteenth century it was the scene of a more crucial naval engagement, the Battle of Lepanto, when a fleet of the Christian powers, in one last united 'Crusade', sank the greater part of the Turkish fleet and so saved Europe, as Salamis had once saved it, from the further expansion of an Asiatic power.

Navpaktos today is no more than a harbour of fishing boats, snugly enclosed within the horseshoe walls of a miniature Venetian fort. Two Venetian towers flank the Straits, where the Greeks built temples to Poseidon. To the west, where already the radiance of Greece grows gentler and more diffused, silhouettes of cliffs and mountains soar up from Missolonghi, where Byron died. Beyond and to the north, confronting the mountains of Epirus, is the island of Corfu, once the rich city-state of Corcyra, with its Italianate air and its classicist relics of English colonial architecture.

To the east of Navpaktos the road winds inland, soon to be overhung by a landscape darker and more aloof, no longer of islands and peninsulas, but of a continent. Mustering in force and deploying in depth, discarding the puny encroachments of man, the serried ranges pile up progressively towards the heights of the Balkan land mass. Through a cleft in the mountains a river swirls down, to emerge into the serene silvery light of a plain, planted from end to end with olives. Continuous as a lake, they flood the land, flowing on into a ravine, then seeping up the flanks and over the limbs of an opposite mountain. Like waves they break on a slope cushioned with grass, beneath a crescent of gold and purple cliffs. This is Delphi, the lap of the gods.

One of nature's thrones, set in a grandiose landscape on the slopes of Mount Parnassus, it was inevitably adopted as a shrine from earliest times. To the worshippers of nature, Delphi combines her opposing forces, joined for once in harmony. Here, to overawe and to comfort, are both the mystery and the miracle. Above, the forbidding crags of the mountain rear up remotely into the heavens; below, welcoming streams spread out at its feet the generous fruits of the earth.

To the ancients, this was the navel, the central point of the earth, proved to be such by Zeus, who sent out two eagles – or perhaps two crows – from the ends of the heavens and saw them alight together here. A white stone marked the spot, and was accordingly worshipped as a fetish, with garlands and libations of oil. Nearby a cave descended deep into the earth, exhaling curious vapours. One day a herd of goats strayed into its narrow mouth, and at once fell into convulsions. The goatherd, following them, was seized with a similar frenzy and, inspired by the vapours, began to utter prophecies. His source of inspiration was presumed to be Apollo, whose 'marble threshold' this became. He had struggled here with the infernal powers in the shape of the dragon, Python, and thus inherited their cult as the Pythian Apollo. A priestess, 'the Pythoness', now took up her place on a sacred tripod at the mouth of the cave, and the Delphic oracle was born. Interpreting prophecies in prose or in verse, her priesthood was to endure for centuries as a major religious, political and financial influence, throughout Greece and the neighbouring countries.

The earliest temple, says Pausanias, was built of laurel, and resembled a hut. Its successor was built of the wax and wings of bees, and was sent by Apollo to the Hyperboreans, the blessed people who lived idyllic lives in an idyllic land beyond the north wind, and whom he visited in his youth, spending a year with them, singing and dancing. The next temple was built of brass, but not, he maintains, by Hephaestus. The next two were of stone, the last built under the auspices of a rich but exiled Athenian family, the Alcmaeonids, who helped to collect subscriptions from all the Greek states, and themselves, as contractors, faced the building with

Parian marble, at their own expense, instead of ordinary stone, as specified. They thus gained favour with the priesthood and, by political pressure on it, paved the way for their return to power in Athens. The final temple, of which columns survive today, was built in the fourth century B.C.

The columns, of a pinkish stone, weathered gold, stand on a high stone platform, sunlit and white, built as it were on the brink of the world. Here once were inscribed the words of the Wise Men of Greece, which became its philosophy:'Know Thyself', and 'Not too much of Anything'. Before the temple stands the altar of the god, where the pilgrims sacrificed; within it, above the sacred but now dried-up spring, was the holy of holies, where Apollo spoke through the mouth of the Pythoness, to be interpreted, in cryptic terms, by the priests.

Below the temple the mountain falls dramatically, forming into ample folds and hollows, spreading its loins, clad in juniper and pine, far down among the shimmering drifts of olives. Behind it, where nature has created an amphitheatre on a majestic scale, man, on his own scale, has repeated it in a stepped auditorium, looking down upon a stage and beyond to a distant backcloth. The great jutting circle of cliffs enfolds it, changing in colour with the light, indeed seeming to glow with a light of its own, incandescent at morning with violets and golds, then with purples and reds, until it fades like the sea to the luminous grey of the dusk. It is the light of Apollo, flooding the landscape with a liquid radiance, suddenly darkened by Zeus with his thundering storm clouds, then as suddenly piercing them with the arrows and shafts and beams of a conquering sunlight.

The Sacred Way of the pilgrims winds up to the Temple, through a grove of pine trees, their branches restless with a twittering chorus of goldfinches. On either side of it are the ruined shrines and treasuries of the various Greek states – Athens and Sparta, Corinth and Argos, Knidos and Siphnos and Syracuse. Treasuries indeed they were, well filled, like the Temple treasury, with valuable offerings, so that Delphi became in effect a bank, with rich deposits, from which money could be borrowed at a fair rate of interest. Only the Athenian Treasury stands today restored. Built of Athenian marble, from Pentelicon, to house the spoils taken from the Persians at the Battle of Marathon, it has a graceful Doric portico and had a frieze, now in the museum, carved with the exploits of Theseus and Hercules.

Works of art abounded. Pausanias records, faithfully, innumerable statues of men and gods, to say nothing of beasts. The people of Corcyra, in thanksgiving for a miraculous draught of tunny fish, presented the bronze statue of a bull. There was also a bronze horse, in imitation of the Trojan horse, from Argos, the bronze head of a bison – an animal caught, he remarks, by luring it down to a slippery slope of oiled hides, then taming it with pine nuts – from Thrace, and a bronze ass from Epirus. The people of Knidos, later to commission the famous nude Aphrodite of

THE TEMPLE OF APOLLO AT DELPHI stands on a high stone platform, sunlit and white, built as it were on the brink of the world. Behind it, where nature has created an amphi-theatre on a majestic scale, man, on his own scale, has repeated it in a stepped auditorium.

THE ELEGANT ROTUNDA OF THE TEMPLE OF ATHENA, Doric in style yet feminine in feeling, hides its ruined shrines and treasures among the crowding olive trees.

Praxiteles, decorated the walls of their 'clubhouse' with paintings by the great artist Polygnotos. The people of Naxos erected a column, with a Sphinx on top of it. Praxiteles carved a gilt statue of his mistress, Phryne.

All these, together with thousands more, have vanished, though they survived the depredations of Nero, who took five hundred statues to replace those lost in the burning of Rome. Some found their way to the palaces of the Emperor in Constantinople, where fire and war were to destroy them. Some survive in the Delphi Museum. The people of Siphnos, enriched by the gold from their mines – of which the oracle took a tenth, flooding the mines when it was not forthcoming – adorned their treasury with a sculptured frieze, showing battles of gods with men and Greeks with Trojans, and this ranks today among its finest works of art. Finest of all is the solemn and erect Charioteer, with his stylized robes, his realistic hands and feet, and his formal head, a statue originally carved in wood, then cast in bronze, with a poetic quality all its own. It was presented by a tyrant of Gela and Syracuse, in celebration of his victory in a chariot race at the Pythian Games.

The games took place in the stadium, a long racetrack cut out of the mountainside, high above the temple, the spectators sitting in seats of earth, until the Romans faced them with marble. Sporting events however were introduced relatively late into the programme at Delphi, when the priests found it necessary to compete with Olympia. Originally the contests were largely in music and poetry. The Greek states sent choirs rather than teams of athletes. Herodotus refers to a choir of a hundred young men, from Chios, of whom all but two died of the plague – an act of God to warn the Chians of their impending defeat in the Ionian Revolt. The most ancient competition was for a Hymn to Apollo. This was normally sung to the lyre, so that Hesiod, who could not play it, was not allowed to compete. There were prizes also for playing on the pipes and for singing to the pipes – until the authorities stopped this 'as not thinking it pleasing to the ear. For singing to the pipes was a most gloomy kind of music and elegies and dirges were so sung'. Later the playing of the lute was added, without the accompaniment of the voice. The prize, appropriate to the love of Apollo for Daphne, was a crown of laurel.

Twin peaks, spurs of Parnassus, soar high above Delphi, creating a cleft where the Castalian spring gushes out between precipitous cliffs. A square bath has been cut in the rock to receive it, and here, before entering Delphi, the pilgrims would stop to refresh themselves and bathe. Today's visitors do the same, relaxing at a café beneath the shade of lofty plane trees, the voices of schoolboys ringing around the rocks, only a little less 'loud and sweet' than in the Delphic contests.

Beneath the spring stands the elegant rotunda of the temple of Athena, Doric in style yet feminine in feeling, the olive trees lapping in waves up to the walls of its ruined shrines and treasuries. Above it loom the cavernous crags of the mountain, echoing with the music of birds and goat-bells. Kept at bay through the centuries by the stone walls of man – here rough and polygonal in the style of the sixth century B.C., there squared and faced in the style of the fourth – Parnassus has yet, from time to time, flung down great rocks to demolish his handiwork. When a Persian force arrived at this spot, detached from the main army to plunder the temple of Apollo for the benefit of Xerxes, 'thunderbolts fell on them from the sky and two pinnacles of rock, torn from Parnassus, came crashing and rumbling down amongst them, while at the same time there was a great cry from inside the shrine', causing panic and instant flight. Up to Herodotus's time the rocks were preserved where they fell, in the enclosure of the shrine, as today are other rocks, the result of a landslide in 1905, which felled twelve columns of the temple. But three columns of the rotunda have been restored, white and gold on a grey stepped base, thus keeping the spirit of the goddess alive here below, as that of the god still lives above.

Delphi lived, as a force in Greece, for more than a thousand years. Initially the focus of a religious union between a number of local tribes, it gradually expanded its functions to the Panhellenic plane, becoming a 'common hearth' and meeting place for all Greek states, moreover an advisory centre on Greek affairs whose prestige and reputation extended to the non-Greek world. Soon the barbarians began to seek advice from Delphi and to send gifts in return: King Midas of Phrygia, who presented his royal throne; King Gyges of Lydia, who, as a usurper confirmed in his power by the oracle, presented the shrine with most of its silver and, according to Herodotus, with 'a vast number of vessels of gold of various kinds, the most note-worthy being six golden mixing bowls' weighing 2,300 lb. The rich King Croesus, his successor, sent even more sumptuous gifts to Delphi – golden statues of a lion and a woman, casks and vases, the necklaces and girdles of his wife. He required advice as to his designs for expansion at the expense of the Persians, and received the answer – evidently inspired by Greek political interests – that if he carried them out he would destroy a mighty empire. As it happened the empire destroyed was his own; but because his gifts to Delphi were 'greater than all men's gifts', the pyre, on which he was expecting to meet his end, was extinguished by Zeus with a rain-storm, and he was conveyed in safety to the land of the Hyperboreans, sending to Delphi, among his final gifts, the fetters with which the Persian King had bound him.

Meanwhile he had founded the fortunes of the Alcmaeonid family. For Alc-maeon, as a reward for his services with the oracle, was invited to Lydia and offered, says Herodotus, 'as much gold as he could carry on his person at one time. Alc-maeon thought of a fine way of taking advantage of this unusual offer. He put on a large tunic, very loose and baggy in front, and a pair of the widest top boots that he could find, and, thus clad, entered the Treasury to which the King's servants conducted him. Here he attacked a heap of gold dust; he crammed into his boots, all up his legs, as much as they would hold, filled the baggy front of his tunic full, sprinkled the dust all over his hair, stuffed some more into his mouth, and then staggered out, scarcely able to drag one foot after another and looking, with his bulging cheeks and swollen figure, like anything rather than a man. When Croesus saw him he burst out laughing and gave him all the gold he was carrying, and as much again in addition. In this way Alcmaeon's family found itself rich, and Alcmaeon was able to keep racehorses with which he won the chariot race at Olympia.'

When the Persians invaded Greece the Athenians sent a delegation to Delphi, to ask for advice as to their chances of victory. Receiving at first a pessimistic response, they re-entered the shrine as suppliants, carrying olive branches, and repeated their question, hoping for a kindlier prophecy. This time the prophetess told them,

> *That the wooden wall only shall not fall, but help you and your children.*
> *But await not the host of horse and foot coming from Asia,*
> *Nor be still, but turn you back and withdraw from the foe.*
> *Truly a day will come when you will meet him face to face –*
> *Divine Salamis, you will bring death to women's sons*
> *When the corn is scattered, or the harvest gathered in.*

This puzzled them. Some thought that the 'wooden wall' referred to the Acropolis, on account of the thorn hedge around it. Others divined that it meant their ships. But the last two lines still seemed to suggest a defeat at sea. Finally Themistocles gave the opinion that they foreshadowed death, not for the Athenians, but for the Persians: otherwise the oracle would have referred not to 'divine' but to 'hateful Salamis'. So the decision to fight at sea was taken.

The oracle gave advice also on domestic and above all on colonial affairs. Lycurgus, the dictator of Sparta, went to Delphi, hoping to secure a mandate for his proposed internal reforms. He received the gratifying reply that he was beloved by the gods, who would give him the best of all constitutions. Many colonies were founded on the advice, direct or indirect, of the Delphic priests who, from their wide contacts, were well informed as to colonial conditions and prospects and did much to stimulate Greek commercial expansion. Often they perplexed aspiring colonists with riddles. The Spartan Phalanthus, before leaving for Italy, was advised by the oracle to found a city where he saw rain fall from a clear sky. Paying little attention, he won victories over the barbarians, but could capture neither their cities nor their lands. One day his wife, trying to comfort him, 'laid his head on her knees, and began to pick out the lice, and in her goodwill it so fell out that she wept when she thought that her husband's affairs had made no good progress.' Feeling the tears fall on his head, he at last understood the oracle, for his wife's name was

Aethra, meaning Clear Sky. Next day he captured Tarentum, the greatest of the barbarian cities, and founded his colony there with conspicuous success.

When Alexander visited Delphi, before launching his great campaign, he arrived on an off-day, when no oracular responses could be obtained. He nevertheless sent for the Chief Priestess and, when she refused to officiate, dragged her to the prophetic tripod. Yielding to his persistence, she said: 'You are irresistible, my son,' – which was all he needed to know.

The Romans did their best to keep the oracle alive, but it died under the Christians. When Julian the Apostate, the last of the pagans, visited Delphi in the fourth century A.D., its voice realistically replied: 'Tell the King the fair-wrought dwelling has sunk into the dust: Phoebus has no longer a shelter or a prophetic laurel, neither has he a speaking fountain; the fair water is dried up.' It was the end, though the Emperor failed to see it. The oracle was finally closed at the end of the century by the Emperor Theodosius, and the prophetic cavern filled in, with righteous horror, as an entrance to Hell.

THE BISHOP OF SALONICA, robed by deacons of Mount Athos in a stole of white satin, embroidered with sacred figures; in one hand a jewelled cross, in the other a silver staff.

THE MONASTERY OF THE LAVRA is the oldest foundation on Mount Athos. In its centre is a church with wine-red walls, white windows and violet, leaden cupolas.

8

Shrines of Byzantium

From Parnassus, the favourite shrine of the gods, the land of Greece steps north-wards, piling Pelion on Ossa and both on Olympus to reach their 'highest heaven'. The peak of the mountain, hoary in its locks of snow, rides tranquilly above the sun-browned earth. Rounding its shoulder, where the olives encroach ever higher on the rock-bound soil, the road passes beyond them to wind through vineyards, then across to an opposite slope. Here, at the head of a valley dark with cypress, is a shrine of the Christians, the monastery of Osios Loukas. Among such monasteries Byzantine culture flourished. Here, within a spacious church of warm red stone, glow mosaics and murals painted in the deep natural pigments of the earth, to honour St Luke and a Christ Pantocrator as grave as some Christian Zeus.

The road then descends into the broad plain of Boeotia, whose rich green corn-lands provided a watery graveyard for the Frankish chivalry of the early fourteenth century. Its soil is so absorbent that, when the crops are green, it can be flooded from the waters of the river Kifissos, yet still appear to be dry. The Spaniards, marching southwards from Thessaly and encroaching too far on the territory of the Dukes of Athens, thus flooded it, immediately before their army. Confident of vic-tory, the French knights and nobles charged, but 'plunged simultaneously into the concealed and new-formed marsh ... Every Knight, in the belief that he had only some ditch to cross, spurred forward, expecting that another step would place him on the firm ground, where he saw the Catalan army drawn up almost within reach of his lance.' But 'no Frank Knight ever crossed the muddy fields: horse and man floundered about until both fell; and as none that fell could rise again, the confusion soon became inextricable. The Catalan light troops were at last ordered to rush in and slay knights and nobles without mercy. Never', comments Finlay, 'did the Knife of Aragon do more unsparing execution.' The Duke of Athens was killed, and only two of his nobles escaped alive – as prisoners.

To the south lies Thebes, whose stolid citizens enjoyed a period of power in Greece following the defeat of Athens. To the north is another battlefield, the historic site of Chaeronea, where Philip of Macedon defeated both Thebans and Athenians, thus hastening the end of the Greek city state and preparing the way for his own and Alexander's supremacy. His eloquent enemy, Demosthenes, performed in the battle 'no honourable exploit worthy of his speeches, but left his place in the ranks and ran away in a most shameful manner, throwing away his arms that he might run faster'. Alexander, a youth of eighteen, commanded the cavalry, and in Plutarch's time 'the oak of Alexander', where he had pitched his tent, was shown on the banks of the Kifissos. He was the first to charge the Sacred Band of the Thebans, who died to a man, while others fled, Philip dancing in a drunken revel among their corpses. But their heroism was to be remembered. The Thebans buried them in a collective grave, and erected above it the statue of a lion. Towering above the plain on a lofty pedestal, it sits there today, with a proud heraldic air, epitomizing a defeat which was yet to lead to a renaissance in the spirit of Greece.

Northwards again the road leads on through the pass of Thermopylae, where the Persians broke through into the heart of Greece, amazed to see the Spartans calmly stripped and combing their hair before the battle; then across the plains of Thessaly and around the foot of Mount Olympus to Salonica, the port of Macedonia. Steaming in a vaporous haze on the shores of its sultry, colourless gulf, it is a city with a permanently incomplete air, bearing the marks of frequent war and destruction. Its centre, destroyed by fire in 1917, is still an open waste; its suburbs an ignoble array of haphazard, temporary shacks. Its streets are tram-ridden, modern and featureless. Elsewhere, it remains in its atmosphere a Turkish city, as it was in fact until 1912, belonging no longer to the orbit of Athens but rather to that of Istanbul. Clambering up the hillside are steep cobbled streets of Turkish houses, their plasterwork crumbling, their latticed bays sagging precariously; here are disused khans and Turkish baths, their domes overgrown with grass; here are markets rich with the produce of Macedonia and Thrace; here is a mixed population of Slavs from the Balkans and Greeks from Asia Minor, moreover a substantial Turkish minority.

But here is the atmosphere, too, of an earlier age, when Istanbul was Byzantium, and its dependency, Salonica, Europe's main centre of Byzantine culture. Monuments of Greek Christian art at its finest, some half-dozen churches survive to recall a supremacy which endured for several centuries. Earliest is the Church of St George, covering, in terms of its architecture, a wide span of history, from Rome through Byzantium to Islam. Originally a Roman rotunda, it became a Christian church, then a Turkish mosque. A fluted minaret still soars upwards from its bold and drum-like walls, while Roman, Byzantine and Ottoman tombs lie scattered over its precincts, side by side. Around its dome, covering a broad round space like that of the Pantheon at Rome, are mosaics of the fifth century, depicting Pompeian fantasies of architecture in vivid golds and blues and greens, with incongruously stern figures of saints before them, while the recesses are adorned with scrolls and birds in a blend of the classical and oriental styles. As early in period, hidden high under the ramparts amid a warren of Turkish streets, the miniature chapel of Osios David glows with a mosaic, similarly Roman in style but Christian in feeling, where amid plants and animals a beardless Christ is seen and revered in a vision by his prophets.

Salonica in its churches illustrates the several architectural styles of Byzantium. Contrasting with the Roman rotunda of St George is the rectangular basilica of St Demetrius, with its two rows of columns, derived from the classic Greek temple. Destroyed in the fire of 1917, it has been rebuilt as new. But there survive in it four mosaic panels of the seventh century: grave figures of St Demetrius himself and others, no longer either classical or oriental in feeling but essentially Byzantine, a blending of both, through the new religion, into a new form of expression in art. Architecturally, the fusion of rotunda and basilica found its expression in the church with several domes of which the Holy Apostles in Salonica provides a later example, and above all in the single domed basilica of St Sophia at Constantinople, of which St Sophia at Salonica is in a sense a replica, on a smaller scale.

Its circular colonnade has marble columns, their capitals carved here and there into the form of a windblown acanthus. Christ, in a ninth-century mosaic, fills the dome; the solemn figures of the prophets surround its drum; the Virgin and Apostles fill the apse. Contrasting with these are the later and freer mosaics in the Church of the Holy Apostles, which date from the fourteenth century. Products of a Byzantine Renaissance, here are the fragments of a Christ Pantocrator, with delicate hands, His Apostles in monochrome, and familiar scenes from His life. Restrained in colour and conventional in form, they have yet developed a humanity and a liveliness of movement foreshadowing the masterpieces of later western painting.

The Holy Mountain of Athos

But the heart of Byzantium, in Greece, is the Holy Mountain of Athos, which covers the easterly prong of the triple peninsula of Chalcidice. From Salonica the bus runs eastwards, through the interminable straggling suburbs, then out into an undulating, fertile, treeless plain. Two monks, with umbrellas and shopping bags, have boarded it. They hang strings of bread rolls before them, on a convenient nail, adjust beards, pat buns and open their morning newspapers, crossing themselves now and then as they read. The gesture is vigorously repeated as the bus, racing another, swerves sharply in front of it, then lurches ahead, the bend victoriously rounded. The road climbs up, through orchards and hayfields, into a mountainous region bereft of valleys, thick with forests of oak and chestnut, beech and plane. Villages are scarce. Beyond that of Anthemous, where blue-washed houses with vine-covered balconies billow out beneath plane trees into a rough cobbled square, the road crosses the watershed into a drier region of pine forest, then descends to the sea, where the village of Yerissos stands amid stubble fields, by a shingly beach.

Here an isthmus, so narrow as to make the peninsula of Athos almost an island, separates a northern gulf from a southern. Xerxes in fact made it temporarily an island, by digging a canal across the isthmus 'broad enough for two warships to be rowed abreast'. Discouraged by a previous disaster, when many Persian ships had been sunk in trying to round the point of Athos, he preferred to bring his fleet this way, keeping it in close touch with the armies advancing along the Thracian mainland. The work took three years and was carried out, by army and native labour, 'under the lash', supervised by one Artachaes, who was 'the biggest man in Persia – about eight feet two inches high – and had the loudest voice in the world', and who, to the grief of Xerxes, died when the canal was completed. Herodotus describes the operations in detail. 'Most of the people engaged in the work made the cutting the same width at the top as it was intended to be at the bottom, with the inevitable result that the sides kept falling in, and so doubled their labour. Indeed they all made this mistake except the Phoenicians, who in this – as in all other practical matters – gave a signal example of their skill.'

Meanwhile two bridges had been built to carry the army across the Hellespont, but were carried away in a storm. 'Xerxes was very angry when he learned of the disaster and gave orders that the Hellespont should receive three hundred lashes and have a pair of fetters thrown into it. And I have heard before now that he also sent people to brand it with hot irons.' The lashes were administered with curses: '"You salt and bitter stream ... Xerxes the King will cross you, with or without your permission. No man sacrifices to you and you deserve the neglect by your acrid and muddy waters" – a highly presumptuous way', says Herodotus, 'of addressing the Hellespont and typical of a barbarous nation.' He also cut off the heads of the responsible engineers. Finally a new bridge was built, the Athos canal was finished, with breakwaters at either end, Xerxes poured wine into the sea, to propitiate it, and watched the troops coming across 'under the whips'. The crossing took seven days: the army, according to Herodotus, was 1,700,000 strong. It ruined the Greeks, who had to billet and feed it. A single meal for the King and his troops cost the islanders of Thasos the equivalent of £100,000, and the Persians went off with all the silver and gold on the table.

A MONK AT DIONYSIOU, where the communal life still prevails. Here there is a busier, more sociable atmosphere than in some of the other monasteries of Mount Athos.

Today the canal is but a stretch of stagnant marshland, amid maize fields and a tangle of blackberries. Here the secular world comes to an end. From the small port of Tripiti a motor boat now plies down the coast to the various monasteries of Mount Athos, the sacred promontory forbidden all members of the female sex. The sea is green and translucent, the rocks whitened by the sunlight and smoothed by the winds to look like blocks of modern sculpture. From smooth white beaches the land slopes upwards, richly clothed in deciduous forest. A bearded monk waves an umbrella from the shore, as from a bus stop; the boat draws in, and he tucks up his skirts to wade out to it, two boys carrying his baggage behind him. The boat rounds a headland, and there before it, with a cluster of monks on its jetty, is Zographos, the first of the procession of monasteries.

'Stately homes' of Byzantium, sheltering, with an eye to a site, by the water's edge or effectively poised above it, they line the coast, each enjoying its own harbour and arsenal and warehouses, its own feudal domain of terraced gardens and orchards and olive groves. Massive as fortresses, they have walls and battlements of weathered Byzantine stone, commanded by castellated towers. Narrow windows pierce the stone, relics of the days when men built still with an eye on defence, and daily life – especially monastic life – looked inwards. But as time went on, and it began to look outwards, the monks built more freely, expanding as it were their castle keeps into country mansions, surmounting the rough Byzantine walls with more elegant stories of light lath and plaster, their windows and balconies wide open to the sea and the world around them. Organic and unplanned, they have grown up through the centuries like towns; refectories, kitchens, libraries, treasuries, store houses, guest houses and monastic quarters, built haphazard around a series of irregular courtyards, with churches and chapels, amid fountains and trees, in the centre. Above all, they are places alive with colour. For the walls and domes of the churches, the plastered fronts and timbered balconies of the various monastic buildings, have been coloured, with a gaiety all unmonastic, in an inconsequent confusion of reds and pinks and blues and buffs and yellows. It is a setting where life has been lived unchanged for close on a thousand years.

Traditionally the Holy Mountain was Christianized by the Virgin herself, carried here by a contrary wind on her way to visit Lazarus in Cyprus. Finding a temple of Apollo, whose oracle bade the inhabitants pay respects to her, she converted them to Christianity and blessed the mountain before her departure. In fact Christian hermits began to frequent Athos in the middle of the ninth century. With the end of iconoclasm they came down into the world from their mountain, as from Mount Ida and Mount Olympus, to help revive popular enthusiasm for images, pictures and relics. The first monastery was founded a hundred years later. It was followed, in the course of a further century, by eleven more, and by the sixteenth

WITH A TOUCH OF THE TUDOR in its chimneys and lichened roofs Vatopedi, most opulent of the monasteries of Athos, is built in a classic style. The blood-red tower of its church looks out over a red and white fountain.

century the last had been established of the twenty which survive today. From the earliest days the monks enjoyed a wide degree of autonomy. The hermits had proprietorial rights over the Mountain, and the monasteries which followed them won wide independence of all but imperial control. The Turks respected the administrative autonomy of the Mountain, and today, under the Greeks, it enjoys its own constitution, prohibiting the alienation of its land, exempting it from export, import and death duties, allowing it judicial authority, and submitting the representative of the Greek Government – an official of the Foreign Office – to the control of a Holy Synod, which represents the twenty monasteries. Sitting in Karyes, the capital, a small cobbled village dwarfed by a large tenth-century church, the Synod alone sanctions visits to the monasteries from the outside world.

The exclusion of the female sex was laid down by Athanasius, the founder of the first monastery, following the rule of the founder of his Order, Theodore: 'Have no animal of the female sex in domestic use, seeing that you have renounced the female sex altogether, whether in house or field, since none of the holy fathers had such, nor does nature require them. Be not driven by horses or mules without necessity, but go on foot, in imitation of Christ. But if there is need, let your beast be the foal of an ass.' An alternative tradition, concerning the rule, is that it derived from the Virgin, who jealously expelled the Empress Pulcheria from a monastery which she herself had founded. In the eleventh century there was a scandal, when three hundred families of nomad shepherds settled on the Mountain and began to supply the monks, not only with milk and with wool but with women; while at times it was thought necessary to extend the rule to exclude also 'eunuchs and beardless people'.

The port of the Mountain is Daphni, a few houses and shops giving on to a roadstead so deep that ships cannot easily anchor. Beyond it the Mountain itself materializes, an aloof grey pyramid, rising six thousand feet from the sea. A giant named Athos hurled it at Poseidon; Juno took off from its summit in flying to Lemnos; one of Alexander's engineers proposed carving it into an effigy of his master; Strabo found it 'so lofty that the husbandmen on the summit are already weary of their labour, the sun having long since risen to them, when to the inhabitants of the shore it is the beginning of cock-crowing'. Hieratic in its gravity, the Mountain falls in stylized folds, like the robes of a patriarch, from a peak like an episcopal mitre. It might well have been carved into the likeness, not of Alexander, but of some Byzantine Saint.

Around the southern point of the peninsula, it drops sheer to the sea in great slats and spirals of tumbling, beetling rock, its cliffs and caverns carved into fabulous forms or, like incomplete sculptures, roughly chipped as by the chisel of a giant, revealing streaks of gold beneath the rugged, streaked red stone. The waves swing against them and into the caves without respite, hurling up jets and spouts of foam.

It is no matter for surprise that some hundreds of the Persian ships were wrecked against them; moreover easy to believe that these raging fathomless waters are, as Herodotus says, 'full of man-eating monsters, so that those of the ships' companies who were not dashed to pieces on the rocks, were seized and devoured. Others, unable to swim, were drowned; others, again, died of cold.'

But on these barren cliffs men in hundreds have chosen to make their homes. Here, perched high on their inaccessible faces, plastered to the sides of them, wedged in their crevices, are the caves and cottages and buts and bens, the retreats and chapels of hermits – Stylites on pillars of cliff – men who still prefer solitude to the too communal life of the monasteries. Beyond, on its eastern flank, the mountain relaxes, now cushioned in green, luxuriant with woods of oak and chestnut, thickets of arbutus and pine, and here, disposed amid well-terraced fields, are their less austere retreats – farmhouses or manor houses where, singly or in groups, they combine the life of devotion with the life of the soil.

Looking down over this fertile wooded coastline is the monastery of the Lavra, the earliest foundation on Athos. From a miniature walled harbour, with a lofty tower, a white, stony mule track winds steeply up to it, between walls matted with ivy and hedgerows tangled with Old Man's Beard. A monk by the roadside, picking lavender to put among his robes, waves a greeting to the passing traveller. Beneath spreading chestnuts the fields are fragrant with new-mown hay, the final approach to the monastery with rose oleanders burgeoning over clean white walls. Beyond them arise fortified walls, containing a rambling 'town'. A battlemented keep watches over it, commanding a jigsaw of roofs dappled by lichens and mosses, their slates glowing warmly in the sunlight. In a white domed porch a monkish porter unloads the traveller's baggage, and ushers him in through a studded doorway. Walking up a vaulted passage, then out across a courtyard and down an alley, he emerges into the principal square. In its centre is a church with wine-red walls, white windows and violet leaden cupolas, around it buildings as various as the homes of individuals in their styles and materials, formal and casual, stone and plaster and brick.* It is the Feast of St Athanasius and the monastery is crowded with visitors.

Athanasius was the orphaned child of rich parents from Trebizond. As a boy, in Constantinople, he became a friend of Nicephorus Phocas, an eminent and pious court functionary, who evolved the idea of founding a monastic community on Athos. Athanasius himself retired to the Mountain, where he lived as a monk, in obscurity. Expecting to be joined as such by Nicephorus, he was indignant when, instead, he allowed himself to be crowned as Emperor. But Nicephorus, partly in atonement for so worldly a step, immediately endowed and started to build the monastery of the Lavra, of which Athanasius became Abbot, being subsequently killed by the fall of the dome, as he was rebuilding the church. Initially, like those

* Plate, p. 108.

which followed it, the monastery adopted his cenobitic rule, involving community of property and a communal way of living.

But as time went on, and a desire for wealth and individual liberty grew, this gave place to the laxer idiorhythmic rule, by which monks could own property and lead freer lives, with fewer communal obligations. After various vicissitudes, this is the rule which now prevails at the Lavra, and in most of the monasteries of Athos. Here the monks have their own sets of rooms within the monastery, where they live and eat separately, and their own lands outside it, which they may own or hold from the monastery as life tenants, benefiting from the sale of the produce, often making their own wine and enjoying perhaps the amenities of a small 'country-house', on the land. They may pay or support other monks, younger retainers, as it were, who help to run their establishments and work their land, and to whom they will often bequeath property at their death.

But on the Feast of St Athanasius the monastery reverts, for a few days, to a more communal way of life. Monks in their hundreds come in from the surrounding retreats to make their devotions to the Saint, to see their friends, to sell their rough arts and crafts, and to make domestic and devotional purchases from the shop in the porter's lodge and the lay pedlars assembled outside it. They gather around the domed fountain, before the church, beneath two giant cypresses, of which one is declared to have been planted by Athanasius himself. Here ceremonies are frequent: the procession of the holy ikon of the Virgin, gleaming silver among the flowing black robes of the monks; the blessing of the traditional platters of barley, sugared and coloured and fashioned into portraits of the Virgin and St Athanasius; a continual coming and going of dignitaries, richly caparisoned in coloured brocades, followed by deacons administering to them, as vivid as attendant flights of birds.

Presently there is the sound as of a rhythmical tattoo, as a monk beats with a hammer on a long wooden sounding board, and all file into the refectory, beneath the portrait of the Virgin, solemn above the outer door. For the occasion the monks have reverted to the communal meals which prevailed in cenobitic times. Projecting from the walls, built into the floor, are horse-shoe tables of stone, with stone benches around them. At the head, beneath a window, is a larger table, where the elders of the monastery sit, as in some painting of the Last Supper, looking down at the seated assembly of monks and visitors and lay workers, filling the hall. Beneath a timbered ceiling, the walls are entirely covered with sixteenth-century frescoes, by a Cretan master, painted on an indigo ground in harmonious earthy colours. Grave, bearded saints preside, on the walls, over the bearded monks, seated at table beneath them. Above them rage the hideous atrocities of Christian martyrdom: pagan assassins armed with swords, heads rolling in the dust, complete with haloes, decapitated corpses still holding them. The meal, which is eaten in silence, consists of a bean soup, dried fish, and a form of sweet porridge, washed down by the monastery's light *vin rosé*, a small decanter before each place. Throughout it a monk at a lectern reads a passage from the life of a Saint, until the Abbot stops him by a rap on a bell, and he is rewarded with bread and wine. This is blessed and then carried in procession down the hall, for distribution among the rest of the company.

During the Feast services are held, not only in the daytime, but in the evening, lasting all through the night. Announcing them, a single bellringer sits on a platform, working an intricate carillon from strings in his fingers and pedals at his feet. Monks and bishops answer the summons, filing into the church, before the sun has set over the Mountain, for a vigil of singing and prayer which will last until long after it has risen in the morning. It is the full Byzantine liturgy, the ritual of a godlier yet more sumptuous age, performed still in the devout spirit of the early church and in a setting hardly less splendid than in the days of the Byzantine Empire. The darkness of the square, domed church turns slowly to light, as the eye distinguishes frescoes, the sombre colouring of their stylized figures relieved by galaxies of haloes; the glitter of gilt candelabra and ornaments lightening the recesses of the transepts; the richness of the screen before the chancel, glowing with icons cased in shining silver; the lustre of the polished mosaic floors, inlaid with coloured marbles. Around the walls, in their choir stalls, the monks stand, black-robed and bearded, filling the church with the sound of Byzantine chanting, unaccompanied and pure in its resonant monotony, while the ritual of worship proceeds, hour after hour, in the centre.

Apart from a library of valuable manuscripts, Lavra has treasures enough to fill a museum – Byzantine reliquaries and crosses, jewels and chalices and pattens – and the finest of these are brought out to play their part in the service: the tenth-century Bible of Nicephorus Phocas himself, its dull gold cover set with jewels and with an austere Byzantine relief of Christ; vestments richly embroidered, so numerous that the visiting Bishop of Salonica spends an hour in the treasury, selecting those he will wear for the various offices.

As dawn filters gradually into the church, the all-night service moves to its climax. The Bishop, noble and refined in a flowing white beard, is solemnly robed by his deacons, first in a garment of pink silk, then in a cope of cloth of gold, embossed with elaborate floral designs, finally in a stole of white satin, rich with embroideries of sacred figures, in the form of a Cross.* On his head is a heavy mitre of white satin and gold thread; on his arms gold-threaded armlets; around his neck gold chains weighted with jewels; in one hand a jewelled Cross, in the other a silver staff, surmounted by a Cross between two coiling serpents. The clergy around him are arrayed in brocaded robes of brilliant colours, from vermilion to crimson, gentian blue to emerald green. As he raises his hand in frequent blessing, he sings in a

* Plate, p. 107.

baritone voice more resonant than all the rest. Many times he withdraws into the chancel and emerges again into the nave, now ablaze with the light of candles. As the service nears its end, in a crescendo of song, the chandeliers are made to swing gently in circles, sweeping the church with shadows, their yellow light coalescing with the white light of the sun, now thrusting its shafts through the windows. When it is over, soon after nine o'clock, the congregation processes across the court-yard to a reception room where coffee is served, with Turkish delight and glasses of *ouzo*; thence to the refectory for luncheon, and so to bed.

The Christian Acropolis

The monasteries of Athos vary in their circumstances, hence in their atmosphere, as great houses do. The most opulent is Vatopedi, on the eastern coast, a large and various complex of buildings, confronting a long white beach (where the monks may never bathe). Approached by a lime avenue, it is built in a classical style, with a baronial tower, a touch of the Tudor in its chimneys and lichened roofs, and of the Regency in its wings, stuccoed blue or a deep *sang de bœuf*.* Thick blue carpets line its corridors, woven with the double-headed eagle and crown, for the visit of a nineteenth-century Tsar. There is electric light and modern plumbing. The guest house is comfortable. Smoking is not discouraged. Visitors are courteously received in a large drawing-room, furnished in the Victorian manner, with couches and rocking-chairs, photographs and portraits of abbots, an *art nouveau* electrolier, a variety of ornaments – a crucifix in a bottle, an outsize lemon in another – and a plush-covered table with a pom-pom fringe, laden with albums. In a church, with a blood-red clock tower and a red and white fountain before it, are frescoes seeming, from the restraint of their colouring, to fill the domes with a diaphanous blue-grey mist.

Vatopedi is a monastery rich in treasures. In its sanctuary are miniature mosaics, finely wrought; a piece of the Virgin's girdle, valuable as a cure for the plague; an icon of the Virgin, framed in gold with Byzantine reliefs; a giant candle before it which is said to have burnt for a thousand years, even when the Saracens flung it, with the icon, into a well. In its library are precious manuscripts of the gospels and the psalter of an Emperor, preserved in glass cases; and a bowl of jasper, a gift of the Byzantine ruler of Mistra, with handles in the form of dragons. On a hillside, above the monastery, are the ruins of a school, a short-lived product of the educational re-vival of the eighteenth century, which led to the ultimate liberation of Greece. The monks took strong exception to the lay elements in its direction and studies, its master was forced to resign, and the building destroyed, perhaps deliberately, by fire. The community of Athos was given more to devotion than to social works in the practical sense.

* Plate, p. 114.

Mules from the monastery stables carry the traveller across the peninsula. Through a farmyard fluttering, in unorthodox laxity, not merely with cocks but with hens, moreover through fields where lambs are grazing, the fruit of ewes, and where the lay workers of the monastery are gathering the harvest, the path winds up through orchards and scrub into cool sweet forests of chestnut; then crosses the watershed and winds down to the opposite coast. Here, asleep by the sea, is the monastery of Docheiariou, a house which has seen better days. Like all but the larger, richer monasteries, it is short of inhabitants. For in a generation the quantity of monks on the mountain has halved. They number now no more than two thousand. The number of lay workers, a race of small men, with Slav or Albanian blood, from the neighbouring Chalcidice, has equalled and will probably come to exceed this.

Here at Docheiariou are but twenty-five monks, as against sixty-five before the Second World War. Moreover all but a few are old men, giving the monastery the aspect of a home for old-age pensioners. Frail and maidenly as aunts, living in solitude beneath roofs coloured saffron with lichen and punctuated with chimneys like minarets, they eat their meals in their cells, seldom emerging except for the services. The long refectory, with its windows looking down to the sea, and its walls, like those of porch and church and corridors, painted with elaborate frescoes, is deserted. The rows of 'flats', with their pink and blue bays hanging out over the rough Byzantine walls, are for the most part empty. The library, housed in the graceful pink stone tower, is locked, its books unread. The courtyards are still bright with flowering trees and creepers, but only a single listless novice hoes the unkempt rows of vegetables, and the fruit of the patriarchal mulberry, down by the sea, falls to the ground uneaten, leaving tell-tale stains, as of blood, on the hands of the visitor who plucks it. In the guest house a melancholy young monk, with a vestigial beard, serves him with lukewarm macaroni and octopus, his fingers stained with ink – from the ink-fish. Lonely, he confesses that he would prefer the communal advantages of the cenobitic life.

It prevails still in Dionysiou, a monastery perched on a jutting rock, just above the sea, its courtyard wholly filled by a church, redder than all the rest, shedding its warm light over the ochre walls of the surrounding buildings. Here there is a busier, more sociable atmosphere, the monks chattering freely, and eating their frugal meals together in the frescoed refectory. In the church are frescoes painted in reds and blues, with an unfamiliar touch of sentiment, as though by some El Greco of a more Italian School. On the jetty the traveller, as he waits for his boat, may while away the time prising sea-urchins from the rocks for his breakfast. The boat sails up the coast, beneath the overhanging balconies of the monastery of Gregoriou, their scarlet railings combining with blue stuccoed walls to make a purple glow, and so reaches the arsenal of Simopetra, a monastery perched in the most dramatic situation of all. High above the sea, inaccessible, it seems, as an eagle's lair, it shoots skywards from a trinity of crags – three skyscraper blocks, at divergent angles, soaring to tiers of balconies giddily perched on towering cliffs of masonry. Close to the heavens, remote from the world, the monks live their lives on this rock of St Peter, in a silence broken only by doves mating softly on the rooftops. Fire, fanned by the wind from the sea, has several times destroyed their church and its treasures. A dwindling but prosperous community, keeping the cenobitic rule, they have lately faced it with concrete.

Strangest of all the monasteries of Athos is Russico, once an outpost of Russian imperialism. Its buildings, erected in the nineteenth century, are as vast and as bleak as barracks designed to contain an army; and indeed that was, in a sense, their original purpose. For the Russians, in their drive to the South, saw in Athos a potential stronghold on the shores of a warm sea, and systematically increased the population of Slav monks until it exceeded that of the Greeks. On the liberation of the Mountain from Turkish rule, they worked for an international administration, in which the Slavs would have the ruling voice. In 1913 they went so far as to land troops at Russico, to put down a heretical dispute. But their designs were foiled by the First World War, and the government of Athos became Greek.

Russico, with its barracks, its churches flamboyant with onion domes and jew-elled crosses, its harbour large enough to berth steamships, survives as a monument to their failure. Its rooms and corridors hang with prints of episodes in the lives of the Russian Imperial family, of Grand Dukes and Patriarchs, of Moscow and the Kremlin, of Russian battles, of the Mountain itself with a fleet of Russian warships sailing around its shores. But they are deserted. The rows of numbered rooms are empty. The courtyards are empty but for an occasional greybeard, shuffling along with a teapot; the porter's lodge but for an aged janitor asleep on a Bessarabian rug. Before the First World War there were fifteen hundred monks at Russico, after it there were six hundred, today there are seventy, of whom half are bedridden, and no new monks are admitted. As a bell rings for the service some emerge from their rooms. In a church, white and gold like a drawing-room, they chant the Russian liturgy in high, cracked voices. Then they file into a refectory, a hundred yards long with an array of some fifty tables. One of them, far up by the window, is laid for eleven, and here, with the visitor, they eat in silence. Another ten years, and they will be no more.

But the Holy Mountain will survive, the Acropolis of the Christians maintaining, over the wide span of history, that thread of Greek continuity, in mind and spirit, which the Acropolis of Pericles first enshrined.

HIGH ABOVE THE SEA looms Simopetra monastery, its three skyscraper blocks soaring to tiers of balconies giddily perched on cliffs of rock and masonry.

NOVICE MONK OF SIMOPETRA. Close to the heavens, remote from the world, the dwindling community of monks lives a life of seclusion on this rock of St Peter.

Index

Illustrations are indicated with italic figures

INDEX